THE WYE VALLEY WALK

Kate and Teg enjoying the Wye Valley Walk
(Drew Buckley)

The Wye Valley Walk

The Wye Valley Walk passes through this beautiful part of the world which I'm lucky enough to call home. Don't rush the walk. The route often climbs away from the river providing a different perspective on the unfolding landscapes that are frequently, and sometimes literally, breathtaking. Remember to stop once in a while and take in your magnificent surroundings.

Kate Humble

THE WYE VALLEY WALK

OFFICIAL ROUTE GUIDE

The Wye Valley Walk Partnership

JUNIPER HOUSE, MURLEY MOSS,
OXENHOLME ROAD, KENDAL, CUMBRIA LA9 7RL
www.cicerone.co.uk

© The Wye Valley Walk Partnership 2011
First edition 2011
ISBN: 978 1 85284 625 1
Reprinted 2018 (with updates)

The first Official Route Guide to the Wye Valley Walk produced by the Wye Valley Walk Partnership was published in December 1996 for the route from Chepstow to Rhayader. The guide to the route from Chepstow to Hafren Forest was first published in 2003 and reprinted in 2009.

Printed by KHL Printing, Singapore
A catalogue record for this book is available from the British Library.
All photographs are by the Wye Valley AONB unless otherwise stated.

Ordnance Survey® This project includes mapping data licensed from Ordnance Survey® with the permission of the Controller of Her Majesty's Stationery Office. © Crown copyright 2011. All rights reserved. Licence number PU100012932.

The Wye Valley Walk Partnership

The Wye Valley Walk is managed by a partnership of the local authorities of Monmouthshire, Herefordshire and Powys, who established and continue to maintain the route and the Wye Valley Area of Outstanding Natural Beauty (AONB) which stretches from the Chepstow to Hereford. It is the commitment and enthusiasm of staff from these organisations over 40 years that has enabled the Wye Valley Walk to be developed.

Acknowledgements

Over the years many leaflets and several guidebooks have been produced by the Wye Valley Walk Partnership to promote the route. Staff from the organisations within the Partnership have written the text, with help from volunteers. The Wye Valley Walk Partnership continue to manage and maintain the route and the website www.wyevalleywalk.org. We would like to thank the Environment Agency, Forestry Commission and Natural Resources Wales for their support in managing and promoting the Walk. We hope you find this route guide useful and enjoy the Walk!

Front cover: Wye Valley Walk at Boughrood – Stage 12 (Michael Mable)

CONTENTS

APPENDICES

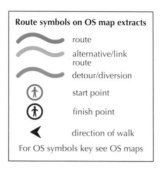

Route symbols on OS map extracts

route

alternative/link route

detour/diversion

start point

finish point

direction of walk

For OS symbols key see OS maps

Updates to this Guide

While every effort is made by our authors to ensure the accuracy of guidebooks as they go to print, changes can occur during the lifetime of an edition. Any updates that we know of for this guide will be on the Cicerone website (www.cicerone.co.uk/625/updates), so please check before planning your trip. We also advise that you check information about such things as transport, accommodation and shops locally. Even rights of way can be altered over time. We are always grateful for information about any discrepancies between a guidebook and the facts on the ground, sent by email to updates@cicerone.co.uk or by post to Cicerone, Juniper House, Murley Moss, Oxenholme Road, Kendal, LA9 7RL. If you have specific comments about the Wye Valley Walk itself – such as issues with waymarking or access – please contact the **Wye Valley AONB** by emailing information@wyevalleyaonb.org.uk or writing to the Information Officer, Wye Valley AONB, Hadnock Road, Monmouth NP25 3NG.

Register your book: To sign up to receive free updates, special offers and GPX files where available, register your book at www.cicerone.co.uk.

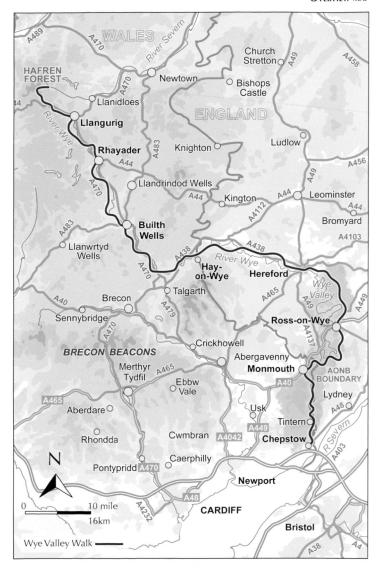

Walking through Beech Wood – Stage 1

INTRODUCTION

Rainbow over the Wye Valley Walk at Wyestone –Stage 3

Dappled wooded glades, eye-stretching views, ancient ruins, towering cliffs, gentle river meadows and sweeping uplands hold the clue to the magic of the Wye Valley Walk. A perfect mix of river and hill walking, it follows the river valley of the Wye north for almost 221km (136 miles) from the dramatic limestone gorges at Chepstow in Monmouthshire to the rugged moorland slopes of Plynlimon in Powys, criss-crossing the border between England and Wales.

It is the combination of the dramatic and peaceful which makes this river walk one of the most admired in the UK. After enjoying the spectacular wooded ravines of Monmouthshire

and the Forest of Dean, the walker enters the more gentle red-earthed farming countryside of Herefordshire with its rolling fields, gnarled cider orchards and historic cattle. The rugged uplands of Mid Wales in Powys then offer an unsurpassed hill-walking experience on the last leg of the route.

Several historic market towns including Chepstow, Monmouth, Ross-on-Wye, the city of Hereford, Hay-on-Wye, Builth Wells and Rhayader can be visited along the route, as well as many small villages and pretty hamlets. The Walk is never very far from roads and houses although the settlements become smaller and more dispersed beyond

Hay-on-Wye. There are a few hilly stretches, but it is suitable for any reasonably fit walker who wishes to enjoy the varied landscapes and natural history of this delightful area.

LOWER REACHES OF THE WYE

The first 83km of the Wye Valley Walk go through the heart of the Wye Valley Area of Outstanding Natural Beauty (AONB). It was designated in 1971 and is unique among the UK's 46 AONBs and 15 National Parks in being the only one to straddle the English–Welsh border. It covers 326km² from Hereford to Chepstow. Woodlands constitute 27 per cent of the Wye Valley AONB and as a predominantly wooded environment with nearly 29km of continuous woodland,

the Wye Valley is more fundamentally natural than virtually all the other protected landscapes in the UK. Over 900ha of these woods are designated as Sites of Special Scientific Interest (SSSI) and a European Special Area of Conservation (SAC).

AONBs share the same level of protection for their landscape and scenic beauty as National Parks. This is especially important for the 29,000 people who live and work in the Wye Valley AONB, and the estimated two million people who visit it annually. The primary purpose of the designation is to conserve and enhance the natural beauty of the area. In pursuing this, sustainable forms of economic and social development are promoted alongside quiet, informal enjoyment by the general public.

Chepstow Castle – Stage 1 (Linda Wright)

The River Wye meanders through this landscape, which has been host to many activities that have shaped the cultural identity of Britain. Overlooking the Wye are myriad features ranging from caves with palaeolithic occupation, Roman and Celtic settlements, defensive structures such as hillforts, Offa's Dyke and medieval castles, secluded churches, reclusive monasteries and pioneering industrial communities. Landscaped viewpoints inspired some of the great British poets, writers and artists and gave birth to the 'Picturesque' movement. Tributaries cascade down side valleys to join the Wye, giving focus to settlements and power to early industries.

King Offa statue at the Circle of Legends, Old Station Tintern – Stage 2

The Walk takes you over or round six Iron Age hillforts in the Lower Wye Valley and the area has a wealth of historic sites. For 2000 years it was fought over, and this disputed borderland produced an impressive heritage of defensive structures including the ramparts of Offa's Dyke, built by Offa, King of Mercia in the 8th century. This is the longest archaeological monument in Britain and influenced the foundations of the modern national boundary. Between Chepstow and Monmouth the route runs parallel to the dyke and its accompanying National Trail, which it meets again at Hay-on-Wye. Later formidable strongholds were the stone castles of Chepstow, St Briavels, Monmouth, Goodrich and Wilton. Also en route Tintern Abbey, one of the greatest Cistercian monastic ruins of Wales, can be explored.

Two centuries ago the Lower Wye Valley was known not as a refuge for wildlife or as a disputed boundary, but as a centre for iron and paper production. Many of the fast-flowing tributaries of the Wye were harnessed to power iron furnaces, wire works, paper mills and rolling mills for tin. Evidence of these bygone industries

Brockweir Quay – Stage 2

can be seen at Tintern, Whitebrook and Symonds Yat. However at other centres such as Redbrook, Lydbrook and Bishopswood very little remains. Fuel came from the abundant surrounding forests and was converted to charcoal in the woodlands before being used to charge the furnaces. Iron ore was brought first from the iron mines of the Forest of Dean, and later from the South Wales Valleys and beyond. Although it is difficult to imagine nowadays, the river was the major transport route for most freight, and was navigable as far as Hereford, although most goods had to be transferred to and from flat-bottomed barges at Brockweir, just north of Tintern. The barges, or *trows*, were hauled upriver using ropes and teams of men and horses walking along the riverbank.

From the 18th century onwards the Lower Wye Valley also attracted fashionable 'Wye Tourists'. Many writers and artists sought out picturesque landscapes and viewpoints. In 1798 William Wordsworth, who loved the area, wrote his evocative poem *Lines Composed a Few Miles above Tintern Abbey* while staying in the valley. From 2008 to 2011 a major Heritage Lottery Funded scheme entitled 'Overlooking the Wye' conserved many of the heritage features associated with the Picturesque viewpoints, the hidden industry, the river connections and also the Iron Age hillforts that dominate the landscape. The Wye Valley Walk passes many of these spectacular 18th-century viewpoints with evocative names such as The Alcove, The Grotto, Giant's Cave, Eagle's Nest, Whitestone, Duchess

Ride and The Prospect. These were laid out by wealthy landowners to enable their guests to admire the magnificent panoramas that the Wye offers.

On nearing Monmouth you will see the Kymin, a circular Georgian banqueting house and Naval Temple situated above the town. Monmouth is an historically interesting place to visit, birthplace of Henry V, the home of Charles Rolls from Rolls Royce fame and scene of the Chartists' trial in 1840; the reconstruction of the court can be found in Shire Hall. On leaving Monmouthshire the Walk goes through another limestone gorge on the edge of the Forest of Dean and on to the iconic Symonds Yat, actually two riverside settlements famed for their natural river scenery and the limestone outcrop Yat Rock, one of

the best-known viewpoints along the River Wye. From here, in the breeding season, you can see peregrine falcons nesting on Coldwell Rocks. The area is also a popular rock climbing and canoeing destination.

MIDDLE AND UPPER REACHES OF THE WYE

The Walk now enters Herefordshire, and further on along the river the impressive Norman fortification of Goodrich Castle can be viewed standing majestically on a wooded hill as you negotiate the 19th-century Kerne Bridge. The Walk takes you over Howle Hill, onto Chase Wood and through Ross-on-Wye – the birthplace of the British tourist industry. Ross acted as a popular base from which

The view from Yat Rock – Stage 3

Kerne Bridge – Stage 4 (Archie Miles)

the 'Wye Tourists' could embark. In 1745 the rector, Dr John Egerton, began boat trips down the valley from his rectory at Ross.

In 1782, William Gilpin's book *Observations on the River Wye* was published, the first illustrated tour guide in Britain. Demand grew so much that by 1808 there were eight boats making regular excursions down the Wye from Ross. The natural beauty of the Wye Valley and its agricultural fertility attracted several wealthy families to settle in the area from the 18th century onwards, and the landscaped parklands that surround their imposing houses are another distinctive feature of this part of the Walk across Herefordshire.

On towards Hereford, the county's most famous export can be spotted in numerous fields along the route. Hereford cattle are very docile hardy creatures which have made them a popular beef cattle choice all over the world, from North and South America to Australia. This area is also cider apple country, looking at its best in May when the blossom is in full bloom. Many of the cider apples growing in the orchards are indigenous to Herefordshire, and some rare varieties have very unusual names such as Gennet Moyle, Hagloe Crab, Handsome Norman and Skyrmes Kernel. Throughout Herefordshire over the past 350 years there has been a strong tradition of producing farm cider to be drunk by the labour force during the following year, especially at the busy times of haymaking and harvest.

Hereford is the largest settlement along the Wye Valley Walk. The city is named from the Anglo-Saxon words *here*, meaning an army or formation of soldiers, and *ford* meaning river crossing. The cathedral dates from the 11th century and contains the Mappa Mundi, a medieval map of the world dating from the 13th century.

As the Walk leaves Hereford the Black Mountains can be seen in the distance to the southwest. Entering Powys at Hay-on-Wye, home of the famous annual literary festival, the landscape gradually changes again as the hills become higher and more rugged. The river marks the boundary for the next 56km between the old Welsh counties of Radnorshire and Brecknockshire, and the Walk crosses from bank to bank before entering Montgomeryshire north of Rhayader. To begin with the river valley is wide

and there are great views of the surrounding mountains and hills, including the Black Mountains and glimpses of the Brecon Beacons. Agriculture becomes increasingly pastoral, with just a little arable farming close to Hay-on-Wye.

This area is also rich in history. Human beings have shaped the landscape through which the Walk passes for thousands of years. High on Plynlimon megaliths and stone circles show signs of early woodland clearance, and there is widespread evidence of late 19th- and early 20th-century lead-mining activity. Romans, Saxons and Normans fought pitched battles against the Welsh along the ever-shifting borders, and stone 'Marcher Castles' were built as defences by the Normans at Hay-on-Wye and Builth Wells. Skirmishes and campaigns continued for years

Hereford cattle at Caplor Farm, Herefordshire – Stage 6

On the way to Builth Wells – Stage 13 (Michael Mable)

with rebel prince Owain Glyndwr attacking Builth Wells and destroying the castle at Hay in 1402 after his victory at the Battle of Pilleth near Presteigne.

Villages like Boughrood and Glasbury developed from small church settlements of medieval origin and were sited at important river crossings, as were the larger towns of Hay, Builth Wells and Rhayader. This part of the Walk will take you close by the great historic houses and estates of Llangoed, Llysdinam and Doldowlod, but you will also pass many small traditional Welsh farmhouses. Hay meadows and pastures become dominant features and the agricultural methods used by local hillfarmers are reflected in the landscape: the sheep spend the winters on the lower pastures close to the farmhouse, and spend the summer grazing at higher levels on the open mountains and

moorlands. Flocks of hardy Welsh mountain sheep and a few herds of traditional Welsh Black cattle can still be seen.

As the Walk draws gradually closer to the source of the Wye, the river is characterised by still, shallow, gravelly stretches interspersed with rocky cascades. The upper reaches of the river run through pasture with oak, ash and rowan thriving on the steep valley sides. The mountain slopes are home to buzzard, peregrine falcon and red kite. You may be fortunate and catch sight of a migrating osprey, or in late autumn spot a leaping salmon returning to spawn.

Nearer Plynlimon there is a growing sense of remoteness and isolation. On a few of the higher sections the Walk passes through open moorland with exposed wide skies and long-distance dramatic views north and west towards the upland peaks of the

Cambrian Mountains and Snowdonia. The grazing is rougher in these areas and dominated by bracken and gorse; you are likely to hear the musical notes of a skylark in the breeding season. The Walk ends on the slopes of Plynlimon, source of the two great rivers Wye and Severn. It is from here that they start their different journeys towards the sea, eventually meeting again at Chepstow.

WILDLIFE AND NATURE CONSERVATION

The Wye is one of the most important rivers for nature conservation in Great Britain. The Wye and its banks are designated as a Site of Special Scientific Interest (SSSI) from the source to the mouth, one of the few British rivers to receive this designation. The relatively unpolluted waters of the river support a wide range of internationally important wildlife so the river is also a Special Area of Conservation (SAC), a European designation.

The Wye is renowned as one of the most unspoilt rivers in the UK. Unlike the lower reaches of many others, the Wye has not been subject to straightening, widening or deepening, and remains in a relatively natural and unmodified state. The river's natural regime creates a wide diversity of features and habitats important to wildlife, such as pools, riffles, back channels, shingle bars, earth cliffs, rocks and boulders. It is home to internationally important populations of fish, including brook, river and sea lamprey, allis and twaite shad, bullhead and Atlantic salmon, which spawn in the main river and

Welsh sheep (Michael Mable)

its tributaries. Otters are widespread in the catchment, and Atlantic stream crayfish are common in some tributaries and upper reaches. Much of the Wye's wildlife is sensitive to change and is not able to withstand pollution, modification to the river's regime or excessive disturbance.

During the winter you are likely to see kingfishers, swans and other water birds, while in the summer months damselflies and dragonflies are common. Of the waterside mammals, you may see mink; the much larger secretive otter is also present along most stretches of the river, but it is rarely encountered in daytime. The limestone cliffs and pinnacles that characterise the gorges of the lower Wye are a significant feature and many rock faces are important botanically, providing a habitat for rare and beautiful plants. Some of the cliffs also provide regular nesting sites for peregrine falcons – the world's fastest animal. You may see some of the many fallow deer in the area, and there are even wild boar (farmed escapees that are naturalising in the forest – a return of a native after 400 years).

From its source in the Cambrian Mountains to its confluence with the Severn Estuary, the Wye changes from a rocky upland stream to a wide, meandering lowland river. This transition is marked by a natural increase in the nutrient status of the river, which is reflected by the diversity of plant species present. The upper river is characterised by mosses, lichens and rushes, while the lower river is more diverse with beds of water crowfoot, pondweeds and water milfoil.

The river is lined by alders and willows along much of its length, with oak, ash and rowan dominating the upper steeper valley slopes. The upper reaches of the river run through permanent pasture, with mixed farming predominant in the lower catchment.

Otter (Natural Resources Wales)

The diverse nature of the Wye allows it to support a wide range of insects including caddis flies and mayflies in its upper reaches, whilst further downstream freshwater pearl mussels, club-tailed dragonflies and shrimps can be found. Birds such as dippers, kingfishers and grey wagtails occur along the river's length, and Daubenton's bats hunt along some sections. The lower Wye is home to large numbers of bats with significant colonies of greater and lesser horseshoe bats leading to the designation of another European Special Area of Conservation (SAC).

WHEN TO GO

The Wye Valley Walk is rewarding at any time of year. In spring the woods are carpeted with bluebells, wild garlic and wood anemones. In summer the riverside meadows come alive with wild flowers. Autumn is spectacular with trees burning red and gold, and the crispness of winter brings crystal-clear views of the river valley.

However, parts of the route can be muddy and slippery during wet weather, the river does flood and landslips can occur. It is always sensible to check on the weather situation and get up-to-date local weather forecasts via the Met Office (www.metoffice.gov.uk).

Walkers should also check for severe weather and flood warnings on the Environment Agency or Natural Resources Wales websites.

HOW TO USE THIS GUIDE

For the purposes of this guide the Walk has been divided into 17 stages which vary in length, from over 7km (4+ miles) to almost 20km (12+ miles). In addition the final section 'Leaving the Walk' gives advice on how to return from Hafren Forest to the nearest town, Lanidloes. These stages will not necessarily correlate to full-day or half-day excursions or, in total, make up a recommended schedule for walking the route in one go. (See 'Your Wye Valley Walk' below for help with this.)

Extracts from Ordnance Survey maps illustrate each stage. However, the Walk is designed to be used with full copies of the relevant OS maps (see 'Maps' below). Grid references are given at various points throughout each stage description as an aid to navigation. Distances are given in miles and kilometres and in the opening information box for each stage the mileage equivalent is also stated.

These boxes also give the start and finish points of the stage (with the relevant grid reference), the distance and an idea of the length of time the stage may take an average walker, an indication of the terrain and height gain to be encountered, refreshment opportunities and details of public transport to and from start and finish points for walkers who are not walking the whole route at once.

The route descriptions, which all follow the Walk from south to north, describe each stage in detail, with

Bluebells at Hazel Wood, Redbrook – Stage 2

route-finding information as well as information about features of interest along the way.

MAPS

The text and maps are designed to make sure that you can follow the Walk without hesitation or confusion, knowing at all times exactly where you are and what lies ahead. In addition, a great deal of effort has been made by Rights of Way officers on the Wye Valley Walk in waymarking the whole route from north to south, as well as south to north, and providing stiles, gates and signs. Most of the way walkers should find it easy to navigate using the book and a map as occasional reference.

However, signs can be casualties of weather or vandalism and their absence may create confusion.

It is important to go properly prepared with the appropriate Ordnance Survey maps – the map extracts for the 17 stages in this guide are based on the 1:25,000 scale Explorer series – and read the section on 'Safe Walking' below.

The full list of current OS Explorer (1:25,000) and Landranger (1:50,000) maps covering the route is as follows:

- Explorer OL14:
  Wye Valley & Forest of Dean
- Explorer 189:
  Hereford & Ross-on-Wye
- Explorer 202:
  Leominster & Bromyard
- Explorer 201:
  Knighton & Presteigne
- Explorer OL13:
  Brecon Beacons National Park
- Explorer 188: Builth Wells
- Explorer 200:
  Llandrindod Wells & Elan Valley

- Explorer 214:
  Llanidloes & Newtown
- Landranger 162:
  Gloucester & Forest of Dean
- Landranger 149:
  Hereford & Leominster
- Landranger 161:
  The Black Mountains
- Landranger 148:
  Presteigne & Hay on Wye
- Landranger 147:
  Elan Valley & Builth Wells
- Landranger 136:
  Newtown & Llanidloes

PUBLIC RIGHTS OF WAY

Most of the Wye Valley Walk follows public Rights of Way, across private land, with some permissive sections (particularly through woodlands). Please keep to the line of the path and follow the waymarks where provided.

The public Rights of Way are the responsibility of county Rights of Way Departments. Please report any problems you might encounter on the route via individual counties' online reporting systems or to the AONB.

Monmouthshire

Monmouthshire County Council
Countryside Service
Tel: 01633 644850
Email:
countryside@monmouthshire.gov.uk
Report a problem on the route in Monmouthshire via:
www.access.monmouthshire.gov.uk

Herefordshire

Balfour Beatty Living Places on behalf of Herefordshire County Council
Tel: 01432 261800
Report a problem on the route in Herefordshire via: http://myaccount.herefordshire.gov.uk/report-a-public-right-of-way-problem

Gloucestershire

Gloucestershire County Council
Public Rights of Way Team
Tel: 0800 514514
Report a problem on the route in Gloucestershire via:
www.gloucestershire.gov.uk/roads-parking-and-rights-of-way/public-rights-of-way

Powys (outside the National Park)

Powys County Council
Countryside Services
Tel: 01597 827500
Email: rightsofway@powys.gov.uk
Report a problem on the route in Powys via: www.powys.gov.uk/en/countryside-outdoors/report-a-concern-with-a-right-of-way

WAYMARKS

The route of the Walk is marked by discs with the leaping salmon logo, which also appears on the cover of this guidebook. There are also standard footpath waymarks with a yellow arrow, or bridlepath waymarks with a blue arrow. If the path is diverted for any reason, such as maintenance after storm damage, riverbank erosion, or

Wye Valley Walk leaping salmon sign

closure of bridges, please follow the waymarks and any temporary diversion notices rather than the map until you are guided back onto the main route. Check www.wyevalleywalk.org.uk before you leave for the latest news.

THE COUNTRYSIDE CODE

Please remember that the countryside is the workplace and home of the farming community, and respect the privacy of those who live and work along the Walk. Do not do anything that will affect livestock, crops or farm machinery.

Be safe – plan ahead and follow any signs

- It is best to get the latest information about where and when you can go. Follow advice and local signs and be prepared for the unexpected. Check the weather forecast and let someone know where you are going and when you plan to arrive.

Leave gates and property as you find it

- Respect the working life of the countryside, as our actions can affect people's livelihoods, our heritage and the safety and welfare of animals and ourselves.
- Leave gates as you find them or follow instructions on signs.
- Use gates and stiles whenever possible; climbing over hedges or walls can damage them and increase the risk of animals escaping. Follow paths across or around land that has crops growing on it. Leave machinery and livestock alone – do not interfere with animals even if they are in distress. Try to alert the farmer instead.
- Do not disturb ruins and historic sites.

Protect animals and plants and take all litter home

- Litter and leftover food not only spoils the beauty of the countryside but is also dangerous to wildlife and farm animals and can spread disease. Dropping litter and dumping rubbish is a criminal offence.
- Do not damage, destroy or remove natural features such as rocks, plants and trees.
- Fires can be devastating to wildlife and habitats so be careful not to drop a match or a smouldering cigarette at any time of year.

Keep dogs under close control

- The countryside is a great place to exercise dogs but it is every owner's duty to make sure their dogs are not a danger or nuisance to wildlife or farm animals.
- On public Rights of Way dogs must be kept under close control, and as a general rule keep your dog on a lead if you cannot rely on its obedience. On areas of open country and common land between 1 March and 31 July dogs must be kept on a short lead.
- Be prepared for cattle to react to your dog's presence and move carefully and quietly around them if possible. Don't get between a cow and her calf and do not panic. Most cows will stop before they reach you. If they follow then just walk on quietly.
- If a farm animal chases you or your dog it is safer to let your dog off the lead – don't risk getting hurt by trying to protect it.
- Wild boar are now quite prevalent in the Lower Wye Valley and can be aggressive towards dogs, particularly when they have young with them, so please take care and again let your dog off the lead if chased.
- Take particular care that your dog does not scare sheep or disturb ground-nesting birds.
- Make sure any dog mess is cleared up and ensure your dog is wormed regularly to prevent livestock infection.

Consider other people

- Showing consideration and respect for other people makes the countryside a pleasant environment.
- Respect the needs of local people, for example don't block gateways, driveways or other entry points.
- Keep out of the way when farm animals are being gathered or moved, and follow directions from the farmer.

YOUR WYE VALLEY WALK

There are many ways to enjoy the Wye Valley Walk and how you do it will be down to your own fitness, schedule and preferences.

If you decide to tackle the Walk as a single long-distance trail, south-to-north or north-to-south, you will need to plan your schedule carefully. The Walk can be completed in about ten days if walked continuously at an average speed, or seven days by the very fit and determined. However, many walkers choose to do it in shorter stages and over a longer time span and take time to enjoy the many highlights along the Walk.

If you have not done any back-packing before make sure you organise some practice outings with your boots and rucksack to find out how much walking you, and your companions, like to do in a day. Then work out an itinerary, to stop at places with a good supply of accommodation (you can search for accommodation at www.wyevalleywalk.org) and easy options for leaving the route at the end of a day if the weather is set foul or one of your party needs to get home early. See Appendix A for some suggested itineraries based on the stages described in this guide.

Alternatively, if you prefer to tackle the route in short sections, perhaps only a day at a time, the public transport information given at the beginning of each stage description in this guide will help you plan. If you are doing a linear day walk, it's a good tip to park your car at the finish point and make the outward journey by public transport, rather than have to rush to make a particular bus or train connection at the end of the day.

For ideas for circular routes that use sections of the Walk, see Appendix D or visit www.wyevalleywalk.org.

SAFE WALKING

Whether you intend to walk 5 miles or 50 it is important for your own comfort and safety to be properly equipped. Stout waterproof shoes or walking boots are essential with good sole grip and ankle support, and it is sensible to carry extra clothing. Waterproof outerwear is strongly recommended. Take layers of clothing as this is far more effective than one bulky item, and you can use layers to increase warmth or to keep cool.

Take a drink and provisions with you as sometimes you will be far away from other refreshments. Regular drinks are important to prevent dehydration.

Carry a mobile phone but be aware that reception varies in some areas so always inform someone of your walking plans and when you expect to arrive at your destination.

In case of an emergency a survival bag should be carried together with a whistle, torch and small first aid kit which should contain adhesive plasters, insect repellent, antiseptic, crepe and triangular bandages and sun cream of a suitable factor.

Appropriately dressed walkers by the Duke of Beaufort Bridge, Monmouth – Stage 2

A map and compass (and the ability to use both) are essential for hill walking. Do test out any rucksack you intend carrying before embarking on the Walk and ensure it is adjusted properly. Leave out any non-essential items and keep weight to a minimum.

The terrain along the Wye Valley Walk varies from steep, rocky sections to areas where the ground may be wet and muddy most of the year. Some parts of the path, particularly in the Chepstow-to-Monmouth area, are narrow with a steep drop to one side, so take particular care when walking these sections especially if it has been wet, is frosty or icy. Other parts of the path along the riverside can be affected by flooding after heavy or sustained rainfall, and in such circumstances it may be necessary to find an alternative route. A few sections have higher-level alternatives if preferred.

Some stages have access for cyclists and horse riders so be aware that you may encounter them. Cyclists and horse riders must keep to waymarked routes and should follow the Countryside Code. Some of the stages in the Upper Reaches are used for motor sport events that could affect your enjoyment of the Walk. To find out more visit the relevant websites or telephone the numbers provided in the route directions.

EASY ACCESS

The Wye Valley Walk is not difficult or challenging for much of its length and there are many sections that can be enjoyed by people who are less mobile. The Wye Valley Walk

Canoeing on the Wye at Lydbrook

Partnership is working hard to reduce the number of stiles, and information about current stile-free sections may be found on the Easy Access page of www.wyevalleywalk.org.uk. There are also 24 Easy Access walks available as pdf downloads from this site.

At the time of print all route descriptions are correct, however the Wye Valley Walk Partnership is improving access for all by replacing stiles with gates wherever possible.

WYE VALLEY WALK PASSPORT

You can keep a record of your journey along the Wye Valley Walk by collecting the WVW passport stamps along the route.

You will find a copy of the passport, which shows the places where you may get your passport stamped, at the back of this guidebook. Simply call into each one to get your card stamped. Once you have collected six stamps – which must include Chepstow and Hafren at each end of the Walk – you can send for your exclusive badge and completion certificate. Check www.wyevalleywalk. org.uk for the most up-to-date list of stamping stations. If closed, please take a selfie in front of the stamping station and send it to information@ wyevalleywalk.org.uk.

Send your completed passports to The Wye Valley Walk Partnership, c/o Information Officer, Wye Valley AONB Office, Hadnock Road, Monmouth NP25 3NG. If you require further free passports please contact the AONB Information Officer on information@wyevalleyaonb.org.uk or by calling 01600 710846.

STAGE 1
Chepstow Castle to Tintern Abbey

Start	Chepstow Tourist Information Centre, ST 534 942
Finish	Tintern Abbey, SO 532 001
Distance	9.2km (5¾ miles)
Time	3hr 45min
Height gain	481m (1577ft)
Terrain	Moderate; two steep climbs near Lower Wyndcliff, and steep descent at Black Cliff, but generally fairly level paths. Not suitable for electric scooters
OS map	Explorer OL14 Wye Valley & Forest of Dean
Refreshments	None between Chepstow and Tintern; hotels, pubs, cafés in Chepstow and Tintern
Public toilets	Adjacent to Chepstow TIC, and Tintern Abbey
Public transport	Bus approximately every 2hr along A466 between Monmouth and Chepstow; stops on request but make sure it is safe to do so

The Wye Valley Walk starts in Chepstow with a climb out of the town along surfaced footways, then runs through Piercefield Woods (which can become muddy in wet weather). At times the path is narrow with steep drops on one side. This part of the Lower Wye Valley Gorge is on a permissive footpath, and due to the steep valley sides and the number of trees there may be rocks and branches on the path. The route continues through woodland and on trackways to Tintern Abbey.

From the car park adjoining **Chepstow Castle**, the Wye Valley Walk follows the path to the left of the castle. The large stone and information panel below Chepstow Castle marks the official start point.

CHEPSTOW

Begun in 1067 by William Fitz Osbern, Earl of Hereford, a compatriot of William the Conqueror, Chepstow Castle occupies a strong strategic position and was the first stone-built Norman castle in Britain. After being under siege during the English Civil War in 1645 and 1648 the castle acted as a state prison before gradually falling into decay. The large tower you pass under is Marten's Tower, prison of Henry Marten, one of the Regicides who signed the Death Warrant of King Charles I. On the Restoration in 1660 Charles II took revenge on his father's killers and Marten was lucky to avoid execution (by being hanged, drawn and quartered), but remained a prisoner here from 1668 until his death in 1680.

Before the Industrial Revolution Chepstow was an important port, hence the town walls seen on your left as you continue uphill. Small flat-bottomed boats, known as 'trows', sailed around the dangerous waters of the Bristol Channel and up and down the Wye (and Severn) transporting iron and wire from Tintern and Redbrook, timber and oak bark, and paper from Whitebrook, whilst importing wine and other goods from Bristol and further afield. New industries, founded on iron and coal, resulted in the expansion of Newport and Cardiff at Chepstow's expense, but this helped to preserve the historic nature of the town.

This stone was brought from Plynlimon near the source of the Wye, whilst a similar stone from a quarry near Chepstow was taken to Plynlimon (Rhyd-y-bwench) to mark the end of the route.

Wye Valley Walk stone marker at Chepstow, marking the official start point

WYE VALLEY VIEWPOINTS

The Alcove is one of 10 viewpoints laid out in Piercefield Woods in the 1750s by the owner Valentine Morris. He owned estates in the West Indies and used his wealth to lay out the dramatic walks and picturesque viewpoints for the enjoyment of his guests. This became a highlight of the emerging Wye Tour, with people coming by boat and carriage to view the spectacular Wye Gorge, heralding the birth of popular tourism in Britain. The original paths were to be walked from north to south, but rearranged by a new owner in 1790 and the path alignment changed from south to north, starting in Chepstow. Nathaniel Wells, owner of Piercefield in the early 1800s, probably added the '365 Steps' and the 'Eagle's Nest' viewpoints. He was the son of a plantation owner and a slave woman but inherited his father's estates and became the first black High Sheriff in Britain. Several of the viewpoints were reconstructed in 2009 under the 'Overlooking the Wye' Heritage Lottery funded project.

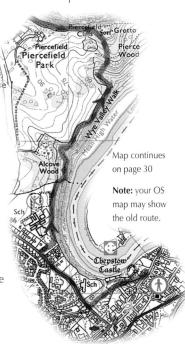

Follow 'The Dell' up the left-hand side of the outer castle wall, following the path uphill. At the iron gates, turn right along the footway passing The Dell Primary School on the right. Take the second turning on the right (ST 528 942 – Wye Valley Walk fingerpost) into the grounds of Chepstow Comprehensive School and Leisure Centre. Go straight ahead to cross the car park, leaving it in the left-hand corner by the Wye Valley Walk artwork. Continue between the school grounds and woodland.

At the end of the path go through a gateway in a wall, and turn right to descend a flight of steps leading to The Alcove seat and viewpoint with spectacular views of Chepstow Castle and the River Wye directly below. The river is tidal at this point and is so until Bigsweir Bridge beyond Tintern.

Map continues on page 30

Note: your OS map may show the old route.

You are now in **Piercefield Park**, an historic landscape, which is private property.

Continue along this well-used and lovely woodland path, which gradually climbs high above the Wye providing occasional glimpses of the river through the trees. Between The Alcove and the **Giant's Cave** there are two paths leading left towards Chepstow racecourse: ignore them both.

Map continues on page 33

The first viewpoint after **The Alcove** is **The Platform**, which you will pass on your right-hand side, although the view is now obscured by trees. The next feature, on your left, is **The Grotto**, a favourite feature in many 18th-century gardens and parks. From the seat inside one would have been surrounded by shells, pieces of crystal and stones set into the walls with a carefully contrived view out over the landscape, framed by laurel bushes. Today laurel threatens to overcome the site.

The Walk continues northwards, now high above the River Wye with occasional views towards Lancaut, a small peninsular community in Gloucestershire which was possibly once a leper colony.

At the second junction of paths on the left, where the path goes steeply uphill, continue straight ahead and down and you will reach the **Giant's Cave** viewpoint.

Giant's Cave, Piercefield

Recent reconstruction work here, including removal of tree cover and repairs to the walls, has made it possible to appreciate the fine vistas which would have been also enjoyed by walkers in the 18th century. The cave was once guarded by a **stone giant** above the entrance, but he has long since disappeared and it is said that Valentine Morris, to amuse his guests, had guns fired from here to experience the echoes bouncing up to seven times from cliff face to cliff face.

Pass through the cave. At the northern cave entrance ignore the steep path to the left (a remainder of the 18th-century walks) and continue northwards, taking great care on some of the looser sections of the path. Cross a stream, which marks the boundary between privately owned land and that of Natural Resources Wales, and after a steep climb up a flight of steps, arrive at the **Lower Wyndcliff car park** (ST 526 971).

At the entrance cross the A466 Chepstow–Monmouth road with care, following a broad track into a quarry. Here turn left (ST 527 972) (or turn right if you have the

The view from the Eagle's Nest

This is the original Wye Valley road, which was replaced by the present road in the 1800s when better roads were required for faster stagecoaches.

energy to tackle the ascent of the 365 Steps to the top of Wyndciff, then turn right), continuing as it bends round to the right, then turn right uphill through woodland. ◀

At Upper Wyndcliff car park (ST 524 972) turn right, following the path as it continues in a gentle zigzag up the hill to the Eagle's Nest viewpoint, the culmination of the Piercefield walks.

The **Eagle's Nest viewpoint**, 214m above the River Wye, with extensive views across the Severn Estuary, was constructed later than the Piercefield viewpoints. It is said it was the favourite view of the Duke of Beaufort who had the path you have just walked up constructed, so he could take his guests by carriage to enjoy the extensive views you are now enjoying.

Your OS map may not show this path, as it is a permissive route through land owned by Natural Resources Wales.

Leave the viewpoint, continuing in the same direction as before, entering a beech plantation after a few hundred metres.

◀ As you leave the plantation over a prominent 'hump' note the change in soil colour underfoot as you enter **Minepit Wood**.

Ironstone was mined here using the '**scowles**' system as used in the Forest of Dean. The iron-ore seams close to the surface are followed, creating deep fissures or trenches in the ground. No one is sure when this was dug or where the iron ore was eventually smelted, but it is possible the monks of Tintern Abbey may have exploited this nearby source.

Continue on the well-used footpath through larch trees, ignoring paths to left and right and following the Wye Valley Walk waymarks. Cross the top of the **Black Cliff**, taking care, where whitebeam (another indicator of ancient semi-natural woodland) grows in abundance. ▶

Eventually the path descends steeply downhill and the surface becomes rocky through a group of yew trees. The path bends to the right then left through another beech plantation to cross a gate into a field. Carry straight on descending gently across the next three fields using a series of gates. Pass through another gate to the left (ST 535 996) to descend more steeply down an ancient pathway to Tintern, passing the restored Tintern limekilns, and for the first time seeing glimpses of Tintern Abbey.

At the foot of this path turn right to join a track entering **Tintern** behind the former Abbey Hotel, almost opposite the abbey. At the next junction (ST 531 999) turn right to the bottom of the hill where the path joins the A466 again. Note the rather unusual seat and the structure of the wall and of the adjacent buildings which show obvious ecclesiastical indicators.

Cross the A446 with special care towards the remains of **Tintern Abbey** and its associated buildings. A visit to the Abbey Visitor Centre and the abbey should not be missed.

Tintern Abbey was founded in 1131 on land granted by Walter de Clare of Chepstow to the Cistercian Order which grew in influence and wealth to such an extent that by the 13th century it could construct the magnificent structure

The tree species – apart from whitebeam – are diverse, and include spindle, privet, small-leaved lime, yew, field maple, wych elm, hazel, ash and beech.

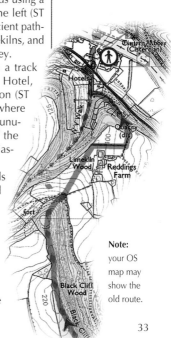

Note: your OS map may show the old route.

33

Tintern Abbey
(Linda Wright)

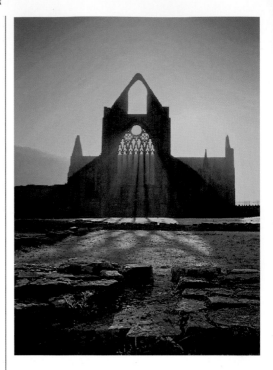

of which we see the remains today. More information on the story of the Cistercian Monks in Wales may be found at the Information Centre attached to the abbey.

TINTERN

Tintern is a small village on the banks of the Wye, but has a long tradition of catering for the needs of travellers. Accommodation and food can be found here, but if intending to stay the night it may be advisable to book in advance as it can be busy, especially during school breaks. There are several pubs and all serve food as well as several different real ales, including some varieties produced locally within the Wye Valley. There is a doctor's surgery opposite the George Hotel and a number of hotels and B&B establishments.

STAGE 2

Tintern Abbey to Monmouth

Start	Tintern Abbey, SO 532 001
Finish	Wye Bridge, Monmouth, SO 511 127
Distance	16.5km (10¼ miles)
Time	4hr 30min
Height gain	340m (1116ft)
Terrain	Forest roads and woodland tracks; riverside paths mainly on pasture
OS map	Explorer OL14 Wye Valley & Forest of Dean
Refreshments	Old Station Tintern (seasonal); pub at Brockweir Bridge; pub at Llandogo; two pubs and village shop at Redbrook; all facilities at Monmouth
Public toilets	Old Station Tintern (seasonal)
Public transport	Bus approximately every 2hr along A466 between Monmouth and Chepstow; stops on request but make sure it is safe to do so

This stage starts at Tintern Abbey, but could start anywhere in Tintern. The Wye Valley Walk passes through the village on the west bank of the river to Old Station Tintern, where there is car parking and facilities. The route then climbs steeply away from the river and continues climbing gently to the edge of the valley above Llandogo at 240m. The walk continues fairly level to Pen-y-fan before descending steeply into the Whitebrook Valley, but from then on it remains almost at river level through Redbrook to Monmouth. Parts can get quite muddy in wet weather and most of the route, although virtually barrier free, is not suitable for mobility buggies. There are three stiles, but two are by gates and can be avoided.

From the small roundabout adjacent to the river and the Anchor Hotel, continue on the Wye Valley Walk on the riverside footpath between the hotel and the river, after a short distance passing the site of Tintern Quay.

Note the archway in the wall of the Anchor Hotel. This was the access to **the Tintern Passage ferry,** and the remains of the ferry quays on both sides of the river can be seen at low water.

When the path emerges again on to the A446, turn right, staying on the right-hand footway. There is a restored waterwheel below the road to your right, and where the Angidy River passes under the road look right and the Wirework Bridge is directly in front.

Map continues on page 39

THE ANGIDY VALLEY

The complex of buildings now housing shops, craft workshops and a café was once the site of the Abbey Mill. The grassed area was a tidal dock, into which small craft could be berthed and loaded between tides. Look across the road behind you towards the whitewashed cottages and note the line of a tramway which came down the Angidy Valley and across the bridge to eventually join the main Wye Valley Railway. The Angidy Valley, along with other side valleys of the Wye, were heavily industrialised from the late 16th century, making the area arguably the crucible of the Industrial Revolution. It was in Tintern in 1566 that brass was first produced in Britain by alloying copper and zinc. The Angidy iron furnaces, fuelled by locally made

36

charcoal and driven by water power, produced cast iron and the Tintern Wireworks, located about 300m up the valley, was the source of most of the drawn wire manufactured in the British Isles until its closure in the 19th century. Wireworks Bridge carried the industrial railway into Tintern to serve the small wireworks. It closed in 1935. A circular five-mile walk, the Angidy Trail, brings the valley's history to life.

Follow the A466 northwards and cross the road to the footway. Tintern is perched on the western side of the River Wye, under a very steep slope, and several watercourses can be heard passing under the road, especially in wet weather. Follow the road through the village, and opposite the road junction on the left before the Wye Valley Hotel take the narrow road to the right and follow it to the entrance to St Michael's Church.

St Michael's Church was the location of a Celtic church long before the Cistercian monks arrived, and could well have been used by King Tewdric, a local Welsh chieftain, who came out of retirement as a hermit in Tintern to defeat the Saxons in a battle close by. Unfortunately he died of his injuries and was later canonised as St Tewdric.

Pass through the church grounds to the open riverside field beyond.

Tintern Parva, which in Latin means 'little' Tintern, was the site of a vineyard planted by the monks of Tintern Abbey. In recent years the vineyard has been successfully re-established and can be visited. The visitor centre is directly across the road by the Wye Valley Hotel.

Continue along the path with the river on your right, and at the gate at the far end of the field climb the steps on to the old Wye Valley Railway track bed. The track bed takes you to **The Old Station** Tintern.

THE OLD STATION

The former railway station on the Wye Valley Line became redundant in 1964, but after lying derelict for nearly ten years was taken over by the old Monmouthshire County Council and turned into a railway-orientated picnic site. Today there is a tearoom in the former station booking office, and the signal box usually houses an art or photographic exhibition. Public toilets are available during opening hours, and a Destination Wye Valley exhibition is based in the railway carriages. A small, basic campsite is situated between the car park and the A466; for rates and availability call 01291 689566.

Continue northwards on the old track bed, leaving the station behind. At the end of the track take the flight of steps up to the roadway on the approach to **Brockweir Bridge** (SO 538 011).

Across the bridge is the Offa's Dyke Path National Trail and the now quiet riverside settlement of **Brockweir**. This was once the busiest port on the Wye, where cargoes were transferred to and from the seagoing ships to the trows. Just north of where the bridge now stands you can see part of the old quay, recently restored.

Cross over the main road, with care, and directly opposite a bus shelter the Walk continues up a woodland path, ascending steeply at first and then more gradually.

The owner has cut a track through the wood to facilitate management of the woodland using the traditional practice of **coppicing**. The wood produced is used as bio-fuel in their home and adjacent B&B. This was part funded by the Sustainable Development Fund through the Wye Valley AONB.

As you approach a small barn turn sharp right up a flight of steps to a track at the top. Turn right on this track, entering a larch plantation and continuing between a thinned area on the right and mature broadleaf woodland on the left. After a short distance the path joins a wider track coming in from the left.

In early summer a carpet of bluebells covers the forest floor here. Note the stone walls and some small **stone-walled enclosures**. They were probably cut out of the hillside to supply grazing for a smallholder's milk cow while the fields around the farm were laid up for hay during the summer, a basic form of transhumance or the 'hafod and hendre' system widely used in Wales up until fairly recent times. Quiet walkers will often come across fallow deer browsing amongst the trees.

Bear right to continue in the same direction, following the waymarked path. ▶

At the forestry turning area continue straight on past a house to reach a road (SO 525 021). Turn right and walk uphill, taking care as this road can be quite busy. After about 100m the road bends to the left, but the Wye Valley Walk turns half-right and passes the entrance to the Scout Association's **Botany Bay Activity Centre**. Once in the wood, cross a wooden slatted bridge and follow the path along an avenue of conifers. After a short distance cross another two streams (sometimes dry). Cross a broad forestry track and continue in the same direction to reach a road.

Turn left and then right to cross the road (SO 525 026) and follow a waymarked path through a conifer plantation. On reaching a junction turn left along a well-surfaced path running parallel with the road to

Map continues on page 41

Notice the change underfoot from limestone at the start of the Walk to sandstone and quartz conglomerate here.

View from Whitestone

reach Whitestone picnic site access road (SO 523 029). Turn right to follow the forest road towards the picnic area and car park. Keep on the main track past a forest road barrier to pass three viewpoints overlooking the Wye. The path continues to the next junction and turns right (SO 521 034), following another track which eventually narrows to an enclosed track. Keep straight on to **Cleddon** and its falls.

CLEDDON FALLS

This has been a local beauty spot for many years and public paths connect it to the village of Llandogo below, perched on the western slope of the Wye Valley. It was near here in 1798 that Wordsworth wrote his Lines Composed a Few Miles above Tintern Abbey. The land is privately owned, but permissive access is allowed to the picturesque Victorian paths which zigzag their way down the slope so visitors can admire the torrents falling over rocky ledges, particularly in winter and after heavy rain. The top of the falls can be viewed from a rather precarious path leading off the main track. Take care!

The route continues straight on, passing between two properties along the unpaved track. The track through the woodland reaches a surfaced forest track (SO 521 046). Keep straight on along the track, noting the view overlooking the Wye Valley below, to a gateway and a narrow enclosed path which leads to a second gate emerging onto a surfaced lane adjacent to 'Moorside'. ▶

The track is known as 'Duchess Ride', supposedly one of the Duchess of Beaufort's favourite rides.

PEN-Y-FAN

The community of Pen-y-fan, where each cottage has its couple of acres of land, is typical of many of the settlements along the Lower Wye Valley. Today many of the cottages show signs of considerable extension and improvement, but previously the small 'crofts' had just enough land to enable a family to be reasonably self-sufficient, with a house milk cow and a couple of fattening pigs, poultry and possibly some sheep. Most of the menfolk would have worked in the adjoining forest as woodcutters or as 'wood colliers' or charcoal burners, as agricultural labourers and even as 'packmen', carrying large loads from the riverbank up the narrow paths to the settlements on the rim of the valley. Some worked in the wireworks and paper mills of the adjacent Whitebrook Valley

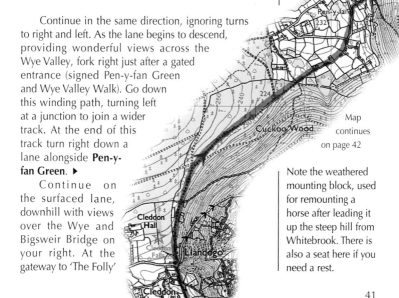

Continue in the same direction, ignoring turns to right and left. As the lane begins to descend, providing wonderful views across the Wye Valley, fork right just after a gated entrance (signed Pen-y-fan Green and Wye Valley Walk). Go down this winding path, turning left at a junction to join a wider track. At the end of this track turn right down a lane alongside **Pen-y-fan Green**. ▶

Continue on the surfaced lane, downhill with views over the Wye and Bigsweir Bridge on your right. At the gateway to 'The Folly'

Map continues on page 42

Note the weathered mounting block, used for remounting a horse after leading it up the steep hill from Whitebrook. There is also a seat here if you need a rest.

41

Map continues
on page 43

the path turns right and descends through a narrow pathway to an open area, then straight ahead down a set of stone steps and a very narrow path to the **Whitebrook Road** (SO 536 067).

Like almost every other tributary of the Wye between Chepstow and Ross-on-Wye, the **Whitebrook Valley** was once the scene of intense industrialisation. Early wireworks were turned into paper mills, making high quality paper from imported rags for bank notes and wallpaper. Whitebrook Farm on your left still demonstrates the size and importance of that industry with the remains of old walls, waterwheel pits and leats.

Turn right and continue past Tump Farm. Note the black shiny blocks in the wall of the farm building alongside the road. These were waste from the copperworks at Redbrook and will probably outlast the softer sandstone blocks used around them.

On the bend turn left (SO538067), and follow the track bed of the Wye Valley Railway until you reach a stile on the right.

The **Wye Valley Railway** closed in 1959 after 83 years of carrying passengers between Monmouth and Chepstow. The opening of the railway in 1876 quickly brought an end to the former mainstay of transport up and down the valley – riverboats and trows.

Continue for about 2.4km when a concrete forest road ascends steeply on your left. Turn sharp right over a stile on the right (SO 534 090) to reach the riverbank, and bear left continuing along this path for the 800m or so to **Redbrook**.

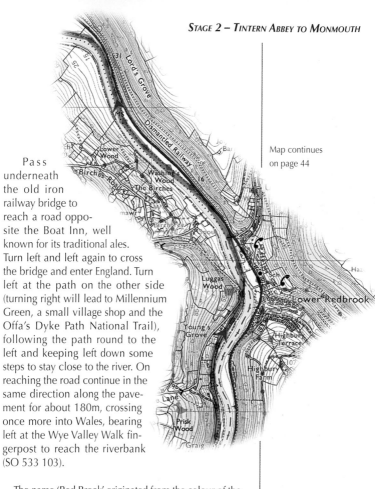

Map continues
on page 44

Pass underneath the old iron railway bridge to reach a road opposite the Boat Inn, well known for its traditional ales. Turn left and left again to cross the bridge and enter England. Turn left at the path on the other side (turning right will lead to Millennium Green, a small village shop and the Offa's Dyke Path National Trail), following the path round to the left and keeping left down some steps to stay close to the river. On reaching the road continue in the same direction along the pavement for about 180m, crossing once more into Wales, bearing left at the Wye Valley Walk fingerpost to reach the riverbank (SO 533 103).

The name 'Red Brook' originated from the colour of the tributary which passes through natural iron ore deposits. **Redbrook** is now a quiet little village, but at one time this was also a heavily industrialised area, with a copperworks dating from the late 17th century, later converted to an ironworks and then a tinplate works. The Redbrook Tinplate Company was world famous for its high quality product and did not close until 1962.

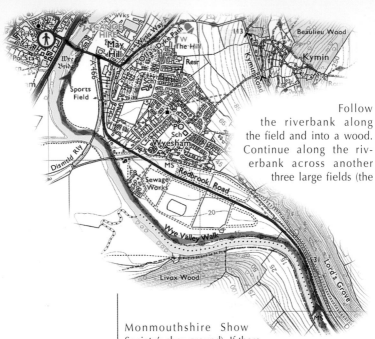

Follow the riverbank along the field and into a wood. Continue along the riverbank across another three large fields (the

Monmouthshire Show Society's showground). If there is an event taking place, keep to the path.

The path continues northwards, passing under the eastern buttress of the Wye Valley Railway Monmouth Viaduct and under the Duke of Beaufort Bridge, which once carried the Ross-on-Wye-to-Monmouth railway. Follow the path around the Monmouth Boys' School playing field. Pass through a kissing gate by the hedge to the left of the pavilion to reach a car park. Go straight up to reach and cross the main road (SO 512 127), turning left to cross the **Wye Bridge**. ◀ At the end of the bridge you have the choice of using the underpass on the A40 to enter **Monmouth** (follow the Offa's Dyke Path signs) or continuing northwards on the Wye Valley Walk, now on the west bank of the Wye, towards Symonds Yat.

The attractive market town of Monmouth lies just off the route and makes an excellent stopping place on both the Wye Valley Walk and the Offa's Dyke Path.

Here you briefly share your route with the Offa's Dyke Path National Trail.

*View of Monmouth
Viaduct from the Duke
of Beaufort Bridge*

MONMOUTH

Monmouth's history stretches back to pre-Roman times; ongoing archaeological excavations have revealed multiple layers of occupation. The Romans called it Bestium and established a fort; the Normans built a castle where the future King Henry V was born, which later featured in the English Civil War. There is a unique medieval gated bridge over the River Monnow, and the trial of the Chartist leaders captured after the abortive Chartists' Rising in South Wales in 1839 was held in the Shire Hall the following year. Three were found guilty of high treason and sentenced to death by hanging and quartering, the last time this sentence was given in Britain. Fortunately, it was changed to deportation for life to Van Diemen's Land (Tasmania).

The Nelson Museum in Priory Street houses a large collection of Admiral Horatio Nelson's love letters and gifts to his mistress Lady Emma Hamilton as well as much information on the history of Monmouth and the surrounding area. Nelson's only other connection with Monmouth was a visit in 1802 to the Naval Temple and the Roundhouse, the whitewashed building on the summit of the 250m-high Kymin overlooking the town.

It is also the home of Charles Stuart Rolls, an early pioneer of aviation and the co-founder of the Rolls Royce Company, who has the rather dubious 'honour' of being the first Briton to die in an air crash.

The town is well supplied with visitor information in the Shire Hall, accommodation of all types, restaurants and cafés, shops, a bus station, banks and ATMs, doctors, dentists and religious centres of most denominations all within a compact area.

STAGE 3

Monmouth to Symonds Yat

Start	Wye Bridge, Monmouth, SO 511 127
Finish	Symonds Yat East, adjacent to ferry, SO 561 158
Distance	8.8km (5½ miles)
Time	2hr
Height gain	Negligible
Terrain	Riverbank for most of way, narrow in places and muddy in wet weather; last section on old railway track
OS map	Explorer OL14 Wye Valley & Forest of Dean
Refreshments	None on route
Public toilets	Biblins Campsite (seasonal), Symonds Yat East
Public transport	None

On this stage the Welsh–English border is crossed no fewer than four times. The route follows the west bank of the River Wye for much of the way; it is relatively flat, and there are no barriers other than gates. Parts can get very muddy in wet weather and others may be inundated at times of flooding. At Biblins there is a suspension bridge with access ramps. The route continues on the east bank on a former railway track to Symonds Yat East. There are no public toilets between Monmouth and Biblins Campsite, and no refreshment opportunities.

The route is only usable by mobility buggies as far as the Welsh–English border, north of Monmouth, and between Biblins Bridge and Symonds Yat East. See 'Easy Access Routes' on www.wyevalleywalk. gov.uk.

Note the **floodgates** on the underpass by Monmouth Rowing Club. These can be closed at times of high water levels to prevent flooding in Monmouth, and under such conditions it would be prudent to check predicted water levels for the route ahead, and not leave cars parked adjacent to the riverbank and rowing club.

From the Wye Bridge continue along the riverside path, passing Monmouth Quay, once a bustling quayside, keeping Monmouth Rowing Club boathouse on your left. Continue along the riverbank, passing through a series of gates and bridges to St Peter's Church, **Dixton**.

ST PETER'S CHURCH

At one time a ferry crossed the river at this point, and the metal gates and steps leading down to the river's edge are the only reminders that the vicar used to regularly cross the river from the vicarage on the opposite bank. St Peter's Church serves the parish north of Monmouth, and although in Wales is in the Church of England diocese of Hereford. The site was probably early Christian; the present church dates from the 12th century, but inside there is masonry which indicates it may have been Saxon. This little church is in active use despite regular inundations from the River Wye, indicated by brass height markers.

Continue northwards and cross the wooden 'Mally Brook' bridge (SO 522 137). Two gates and two long fields later you enter woodland. Follow the well-defined path, passing wooden steps on your left which give access to the Dixton Embankment Nature Reserve, owned by Gwent Wildlife Trust. This was formed when the present A40 was constructed and the route of the old Monmouth-to-Ross-on-Wye

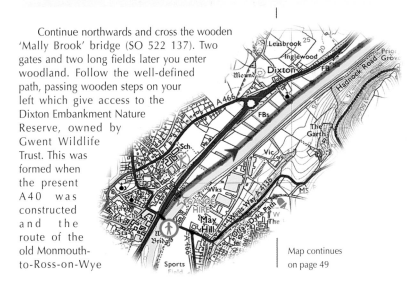

Map continues on page 49

The view from the Wye Bridge, Monmouth

If the weather is hot, you may come upon adders basking in the sunlight.

road abandoned, making the area available for a Nature Reserve. ◀

Sixty metres on and you cross the border into the county of Herefordshire. Continue into England and the path narrows alongside a cottage and follows the boundary of the cottage to a path overlooking the river through the woods. Pass a footpath on your left which rises steeply uphill towards the old road and beyond to the A40.

WYASTONE LEYS

Wyastone Leys was originally built in 1795 and rebuilt in the 1830s by industrialist Richard Blakemore. He extended the estate to include the Little Doward hillfort behind enhancing it with landscaped viewpoints, an iron tower folly, carriage drives and a walled deer park. A later owner extended the house further in 1860–61 by the Scottish architect, William Burns. A small herd of fallow deer are still kept in a reserve on the edge of the Little Doward. Since the early 1970s the Wyastone Estate has been the home of Nimbus Records, one of the pioneers of Compact Disc manufacturing and recording.

The path eventually emerges on to a meadow under **Wyastone Leys**, a large country house.

Please keep to the riverside path through the property – and by the way, you are back in Wales. At the end of the meadow, pass under a pollarded sycamore tree and through a signposted gap and you are, once again, in England.

The path continues past Fishermans Cottage, but at the end of the garden be careful of the iron mooring post with mooring ring still attached. This was where the fishermen's boat would have been moored. The fishermen in this case would have been guests or members of the estate fishing for the prime salmon the Wye was once famous for. ▶

You now enter Woodland Trust land including 82ha of woodland and the Little Doward hillfort (open to the public). At this point you have a choice of routes: continue straight on following the riverside path or deviate to a kissing gate to your left. This path runs inside the wood but parallel

Map continues on page 50

In the fence left is a metal kissing gate high enough to keep out deer, an echo from the past when the deer park extended this far.

49

to the riverside path and leads up to a recently restored limekiln. The paths converge further on at a kissing gate adjacent to an old iron field gate. Note the size of the stone gateposts.

Continue along the riverside path until you reach the site of old quarries on your left. Old tailing (waste rock) heaps are very evident and a short walk into the quarries will take you to the rock wall. This rock face is known as the '**Seven Sisters Rocks**'. Limestone from this rock face was shipped down stream by riverboats, for building purposes and for making lime.

Above are **King Arthur's Caves**; although links to the mythical king are unlikely, evidence has been found of man's presence from 12,000 years ago, before the last ice age, along with the remains of mammoth, woolly rhinoceros and sabre tooth tiger. Today these caves are home to some of our most endangered bats, the lesser and greater horseshoe.

Continue along this path to a split in the route. Take the right-hand path and this takes you almost immediately into the open space of the Forestry Commission's **Biblins Campsite**. This site is for use by youth groups and during summer becomes very busy, so follow the route towards a hard-surfaced path which passes a toilet block for the campsite. ◄

Part of the block is open to the public from March to October.

Follow the track till you reach **Biblins Bridge** (SO 549 144). This suspension bridge replaces an earlier version and is now approached by ramps, but the bridge is still narrow and does sway. (If you feel uneasy about using the bridge, the **alternative** is to continue along the path towards Symonds Yat West, past the ruins of the New Weir forge and take the road right, down to the ferry to cross the river. The ferry is a

Biblins Bridge

hand-operated rope ferry run by the Saracen's Head Inn in Symonds Yat East directly opposite the ferry point. Wait by the ferry until the operator sees you,

51

or if at night, shine a torch and they will come for you, but beware they do not operate after 11pm or in high river conditions. There is a modest charge for the ferry.)

Cross the Biblins Bridge and turn left. You are now back in Monmouthshire, Wales.

Directly opposite the end of the bridge is **Lady Park Wood**, a National Nature Reserve. The form of 'management' is 'non-intervention', and since the 1940s it has been left alone and studied to see how natural woodland develops over a period of time.

Roger was the Wye Valley AONB Cycle Routes Officer who tragically died aged 59, before the cycleway was completed.

Immediately on turning left on to what was the Monmouth-to-Ross-on-Wye Railway track bed – and is now the Peregrine Path cycle route – is the Roger Withers Memorial seat. ◄

Continue along the track bed, crossing into England and Gloucestershire then Herefordshire yet again, until you reach a car park, once the old **Symonds Yat** railway station.

NEW WEIR IRONWORKS

The river here is very popular with canoeists, the rapids being ideal for training novices. In the 17th century a weir was built here to divert water to an ironworks on the opposite bank. The New Weir ironworks were in use from at least the 1590s up until the 1800s. It had various forges, mills and hammers powered by water wheels for refining iron from nearby furnaces. The rapids are formed from the collapsed weir and slag heaps from the ironworks. The rapids have been purchased by the British Canoe Union and were remodelled in 2009. The site was surveyed in 2009 and consolidated in 2010 as part of the AONB 'Overlooking the Wye' scheme funded by the Heritage Lottery Fund.

Continue through the car park, but if you wish to visit **Yat Rock** viewpoint take the very steep footpath between the entrances of the Royal Lodge and Forest View Hotels. The Wye Valley Walk continues through Symonds Yat East.

Symonds Yat (East)

SYMONDS YAT (EAST)

There are several hotels, cafés and the Saracen's Head Inn for accommodation and refreshments. There are public toilets adjacent to the car park opposite the Saracen's Head, but these may not be open between November and April. Similarly some of the cafés close for the winter. Note both car parks are Pay & Display.

STAGE 4
Symonds Yat to Kerne Bridge

Start	Symonds Yat East, adjacent to ferry, SO 561 158
Finish	Kerne Bridge car park, adjacent to Bishopswood Village Hall, SO 581 189
Distance	12.3km (7½ miles)
Time	3hr 20min
Height gain	50m (155ft)
Terrain	Steep climb to Huntsham Hill; descent to riverbank, then riverbank path to Kerne Bridge
OS map	Explorer OL14 Wye Valley & Forest of Dean
Refreshments	Youth Hostel at Welsh Bicknor (opening times vary); pubs at Kerne Bridge and Lydbrook (just south of route)
Public toilets	Symonds Yat East, Bishopswood Village Hall
Public transport	Buses between Ross-on Wye and Monmouth pass Kerne Bridge

At the time of going to print, Lydbrook Bridge (SO 587 176) is closed and a diversion is in place via Huntsham Bridge (SO 567 182). This route may not appear on OS mapping.

This stage starts with a steep climb to a forestry access road around Huntsham Hill, followed by a steep and sometimes slippery and rocky path down to the banks of the Wye where the diversion route begins. A gentle walk through riverside fields leads to Huntsham Bridge where the river is crossed and the route continues beside the river to Kerne Bridge.

From the Saracen's Head Inn by the ferry the route turns left into a car park and campsite, and follows the riverbank, continuing through fields to reach a **ferry point** opposite The Old Ferry Inn. Turn right across the field towards the road, then left along the road for just under 40m, before taking the path right, uphill, through woodland.

There is a large outcrop of quartz conglomerate above the path, where it emerges on the next road. This rock looks like concrete and consists of small pebbles of

The view from Huntsham Hill

quartz and igneous rock embedded in naturally formed sandy cement.

Turn left down the road here for 65m, and then take the path right up into the woodland. After just over 180m the footpath joins a forestry track, which winds its way around **Huntsham Hill**, with good views northwards to Goodrich. At the top of the incline, where the track swings right, the path descends off to the left (SO 565 169) initially down a flight of steps, through moss-covered boulders and fern-clad slopes.

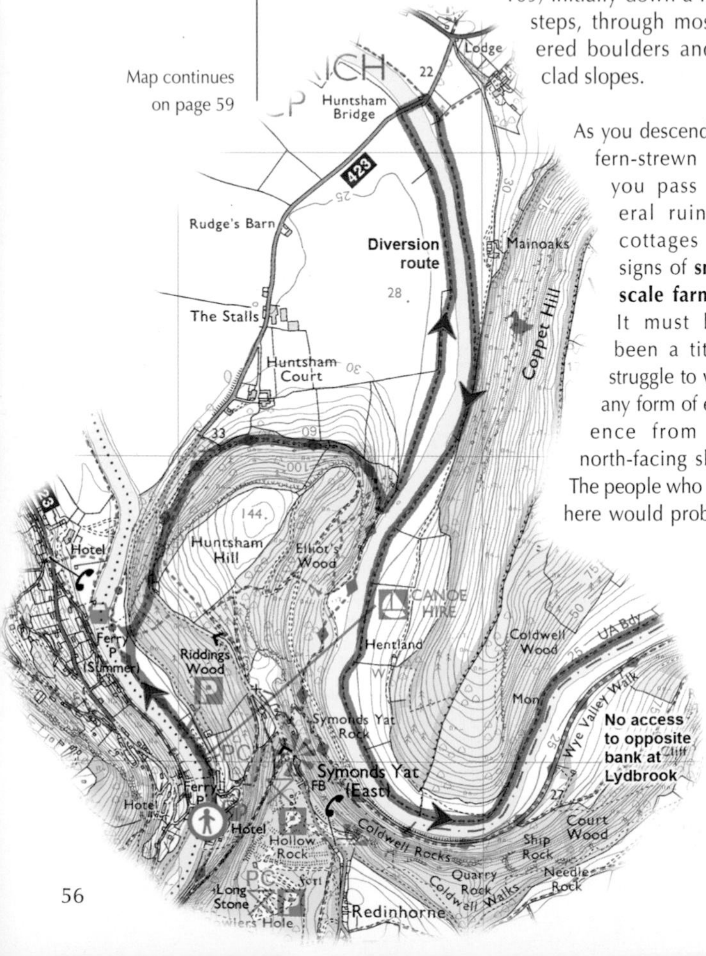

As you descend this fern-strewn path you pass several ruins of cottages and signs of **small-scale farming**. It must have been a titanic struggle to wrest any form of existence from this north-facing slope. The people who lived here would probably

Map continues on page 59

[Map showing the area around Huntsham Hill, Huntsham Bridge, Huntsham Court, Symonds Yat (East), Coldwell Rocks, Coppet Hill, and the Wye Valley Walk route. Labels include: Lodge, Huntsham Bridge, 423, Rudge's Barn, Diversion route, Mainoaks, The Stalls, Huntsham Court, Coppet Hill, Huntsham Hill, Elliot's Wood, Hotel, Ferry P (Summer), Riddings Wood, CANOE HIRE, Hentland, Coldwell Wood, Ferry P, Symonds Yat Rock, Symonds Yat (East), Hollow Rock, Long Stone, Redinhorne, Coldwell Rocks, Quarry Rock, Coldwell Walks, Ship Rock, Needle Rock, Court Wood, Wye Valley Walk, No access to opposite bank at Lydbrook, 144, Hotel]

COPPETT HILL COMMON

To the left the large area of rocky, scrub-covered land is Coppett Hill Common, a Local Nature Reserve. This 100ha common is owned by the members of the Coppett Hill Common Trust Ltd. In 1985 local residents bought the common with financial assistance from the County Council and local parish councils. The Trust manage the common and have established permissive footpaths to supplement the public footpaths which cross the common.

have worked quarrying the local hillside or on the Courtfield Estate.

Reaching a junction just above the river, turn left and cross a stile into fields following the riverside footpath downstream to Huntsham Bridge (SO 567 182). Cross the Wye using this narrow road bridge and then turn right after the house, through two gates, and into the field

PEREGRINE FALCONS

Look up for an excellent view of Coldwell Rocks, home to ravens and peregrine falcons. The latter were at one time on the verge of extinction in Britain due to the effects of the insecticide DDT which made the eggshells too brittle to survive the rigours of a nest. Since the banning of DDT (and with legal protection) peregrine falcons are now becoming much more common. The original pair  which nested here in the 1970s became the focal point of a conservation programme: the Royal Society for the Protection of Birds (RSPB) set up an observation point on Yat Rock and this became a popular visitor attraction. The RSPB provides telescopes for the public to view the nest site during the nesting season, and this programme was directly instrumental in drawing the plight of these birds to the public. The falcons are now a common sight in many cities where they have chosen to adopt high-rise buildings as suitable substitute cliffs on which to nest.

to follow the riverside footpath upstream all the way to Lydbrook Bridge.

Symonds Yat Rock towers above the river and from the late 1700s Wye tourists would disembark on the opposite bank and climb up to Yat Rock to enjoy the spectacular views. Their boats navigated the large river meander to rejoin them at Symonds Yat East.

The factory in **Lydbrook** once employed over a thousand people and produced electrical cable. During World War I it supplied nearly all the field telephone cable used on the battlefields and in the rear areas. During World War II it produced the fine wire used in the heated jackets of fighter pilots and bomber crew. Unfortunately the factory has gone through a series of downturns and is currently derelict, awaiting a new use.

Canoeing at Lydbrook

At the end of the bridge there is the entrance to another railway tunnel and a WWII pillbox (machine-gun post). Turn right here along the river-bank.

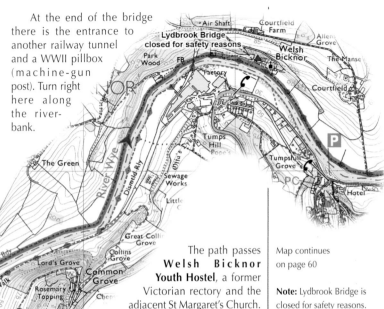

The path passes **Welsh Bicknor Youth Hostel**, a former Victorian rectory and the adjacent St Margaret's Church. The footpath continues along the riverbank through several fields.

Map continues on page 60

Note: Lydbrook Bridge is closed for safety reasons.

Courtfield, home of the Vaughan family for centuries, can be seen on top of the rise to the left. The Vaughans were one of the premier Roman Catholic families in the area and suffered persecution, but retained their lands despite this. The infant King Henry V spent most of his younger life here, having been sent by his father to escape 'the foul air of Monmouth'. In recent years it served as a convent and as a Roman Catholic centre, but at the time of writing it was for sale.

Continue along the riverbank, passing through **Thomas Wood**. The path at one stage is below and parallel to the former railway, which emerged from the tunnel in Thomas Wood and crossed the river by a bridge. Only the bridge abutments remain, adjoining the path.

As you emerge from the woodland the red sandstone mass of Goodrich Castle appears on the skyline as the path continues along the riverbank towards the stone arches of **Kerne Bridge** (SO 580 192).

Climb the steps to the bridge, taking care on this busy corner, and cross over the river.

At the T-junction turn right along a path parallel with the B4234 road. After passing the former Kerne Bridge railway station and the new Bishopswood Village Hall, go left to reach a bus shelter. The route crosses the road here; however, if you continue for a few metres you will come to a car park, canoe launch site and picnic area.

There are publicly accessible toilets in the village hall, and accommodation options in both Kerne Bridge and at Lydbrook (just south of the route); see Appendix C.

GOODRICH CASTLE

Goodrich Castle (Michael Mable)

Goodrich Castle stands on a ridge guarding an important river crossing, now superseded by Kerne Bridge. The original castle, built of local red sandstone, was started by Godric, an English thegn or earl, from whom it took its name in the 11th century. After the Norman invasion of 1066 the Normans took possession and extended this splendid example of castle construction. Amongst its owners have been Richard de Clare or 'Strongbow' and William Marshal, Earl of Pembroke, who was one of the most powerful men in the nation. Eventually passing to William de Valance after 1245, the castle held a prominent role in the life of the Welsh Marches.

During the English Civil War it was held alternately by both sides. The most decisive factor in its surrender to the Parliamentarian forces in 1646 was the presence of 'Roaring Meg', a large mortar or high trajectory cannon, which started to demolish the walls. 'Roaring Meg' can still be seen in the castle, having returned after 350 years' absence. The castle is managed by English Heritage and is open to the public with a visitor centre, café and toilets.

STAGE 5
Kerne Bridge to Ross-on-Wye

Start	Kerne Bridge car park, adjacent to Bishopswood Village Hall, SO 581 189
Finish	Ross-on-Wye, outside Hope and Anchor Inn, SO 596 242
Distance	8.7km (5½ miles)
Time	4hr 30mins
Height gain	361m (1185ft)
Terrain	Several quite steep climbs; much of route through woodland, with urban walking through Ross-on-Wye
OS map	Explorers OL14 Wye Valley & Forest of Dean, 189 Hereford and Ross-on-Wye
Refreshments	None on route: pubs, cafés and restaurants in Ross-on-Wye
Public toilets	Adjacent to finish
Public transport	Buses between Ross-on Wye and Monmouth pass Kerne Bridge

This stage of the route is a pleasant mix of woodland and farmland walking in low hills overlooking the Wye with a short steep climb to a hillfort, and urban section through Ross-on-Wye. There are several stiles.

Walk up the lane opposite the bus shelter for just over 10m, then turn left and go up the first driveway. To the rear of Falcon House take the steps on your right and go up to the next drive.

At the next junction of tracks continue straight uphill. Some of the surroundings, such as walls and trees, suggest this may have been a bridleway or track, though it is only registered as a footpath now. At the end of the path turn left and continue between two houses.

At this point the main route continues off to the left (SO 582 192).

Go downhill for several hundred metres, passing Cherry Tree Cottage on the right. Just before meeting the road turn right and head back uphill (SO 586 197), following a concrete drive. ▶ As the path levels out at the top of the hill you enter woodland which has been coppiced, and bluebells flourish in spring. After passing through the wood, cross straight over the tarmac drive following the path running in front of the old stone wall.

The concrete surface is treacherous in wet conditions.

Coppicing is an extremely old woodland management technique, whereby woodland – mainly of hazel and ash – was harvested on a 12–20 year rotation. The tree growth is cut back to the stump and the timber used for making charcoal, small timber items and tool handles. In modern times the produce has little commercial value but coppicing is used as a conservation measure to ensure the continuation of species such as dormice and invertebrates, and can still produce charcoal and bean poles. Many species of butterfly can only exist in coppice woodland and have suffered decline over the last 50 years.

Map continues on page 65

Continue straight on inside the edge of the wood. The next

road you meet ascends **Bull's Hill** (SO 596 204). Cross it and take the path which runs immediately to the

63

The stream here runs even in the driest summers.

left of the first house on your left (Linden Lea). Follow the path through the garden to the field below.

Bear left to the bottom corner of the field. ◄ Climb up the field, and cross the stile. The path shortly leads to the road on **Howle Hill** (SO 598 206). Cross it and proceed along the bridleway ahead. Ignore steps going downhill opposite the first house on the right. Carry on up the lane past another house on the right. Follow the track around to the right at Still Meadow House, which is on the left of the route; turn left.

At the next cottage leave the track by turning sharp left through a pedestrian gate.

There are some prominent **anthills** developing here. This is a sign of well-established and undisturbed permanent grassland, an important habitat. These anthills are frequently attacked by green woodpeckers looking to eat the eggs and larvae.

Chase Woods (Michael Mable)

At the other side of the meadow, head right under some fine old oak and beech trees. After several gates you emerge on to the road at **Coughton**. Turn left here and

then right through the first farmyard (SO 600 211), going through a seriws of pedestrian gates and up the edge of the field to the wood. You are starting the climb on to **Chase Wood Hill** here. Follow the path up through the wood. Turn right on meeting the next track which soon emerges on top of the hill.

Here forestry tracks meet around a large redwood tree (SO 602 219).

The top of the hill is the site of an Iron Age fort which covers about 11.25ha. The adjacent Penyard Park gets its name from the Welsh 'penyard' meaning 'high hill'.

Follow the track straight ahead and down to **Hill Farm**. Take the entrance into Merrivale Wood directly in front of you.

Merrivale Wood is managed as a nature reserve by the Herefordshire Nature Trust. The reserve of about 4ha is on a north-facing slope overlooking Ross-on-Wye and consists of mainly sessile oak and ash with a variety of other species and a healthy understorey of holly and hazel, with hawthorn and field maple.

At the end of the wood, by a memorial seat, go through a kissing gate and carry on in the same direction. At the next oak turn left and follow the track around to the right through a further two gates into Tank Meadow (SO 607 231), so

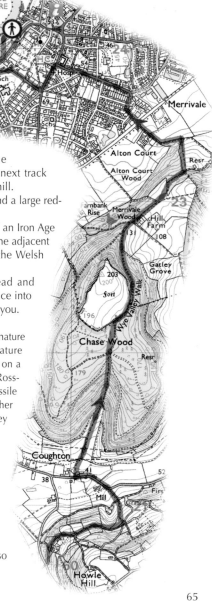

named after the 19th-century reservoir at the top, which supplies the town of Ross below.

Stay on the left of the field and at the bottom turn left through an obscured kissing gate. The timber-framed building reached shortly is **Alton Court**, now the head-quarters of PGL adventure holidays.

Continue along the lane, joining Penyard Lane, and at the junction with Alton Street (SO 603 237) turn left and stay on the left-hand footway until the brow of the hill. Where the footpath runs out cross to the other side of the road, taking care of the traffic, and continue. After passing the **Ross-on-Wye Community Hospital** cross Copse Cross Street into Old Maids Lane, passing the Copse Cross Toll Gate (the thatched cottage) on the left and the police station on the right. At the end of Old Maids Lane cross Church Street and enter the grounds of St Mary's Church. Take the path half-right, passing to the left of the church. The large gates to the left lead into The Prospect gardens with a viewpoint overlooking the Wye Valley to the west of Ross-on-Wye.

St Mary the Virgin is the parish church of Ross-on-Wye and originates from 1316. It is the largest parish church in Herefordshire and has many memorials includ-ing the grave of John Kyrle, 'The Man of Ross', who developed the water supply for Ross and laid out The Prospect in 1700. When The Prospect wall collapsed in 2007 it revealed a possible Roman tower underneath. The area was already known to be the site of a medie-val bishop's palace, but archaeological finds dated the structure to the 3rd or 4th century AD.

Return to the church and pass round to the north door. With your back to the door take the pathway half-right passing the Plague Cross, commemorating the 315 citizens of Ross who died in the outbreak of plague in 1637 and were buried in a common grave close by.

Drop down the steps into Church Street. Opposite are the Tudor almshouses built of local red sandstone and repaired in 1575. Turn left and descend Church Street to meet High Street. You are now close to the centre of **Ross**. Turn right and visit the Market House or turn left and continue along High Street to Wye Street.

ROSS-ON-WYE

Ross-on-Wye has been a market town for hundreds of years, so around 1650 (just before the outbreak of the English Civil War) the Duchess of Somerset, the Lady of the Manor at the time, paid for a Market House to be built of the local red sandstone and Forest of Dean oak.

From the leaping salmon sculpture in front of The Man of Ross PH descend Wye Street. Do not take the steps directly in front but turn left down Wye Street and take the next set of steps on the right, down to the Hope and Anchor Inn which marks the end of this stage.

Leaping salmon sculpture

STAGE 6
Ross-on-Wye to Fownhope

Start	Ross-on-Wye, outside Hope and Anchor Inn, SO 596 242
Finish	Fownhope, 700m from village centre, SO 581 351
Distance	17.2km (10½ miles)
Time	6hr
Height gain	315m (1033ft)
Terrain	Riverside paths, field edges; short stretches along quiet country lanes
OS map	Explorer 189 Hereford & Ross-on-Wye
Refreshments	None between Ross and Fownhope
Public toilets	None between Ross and Fownhope
Public transport	None between Ross and Fownhope; on limited days Fownhope can be reached by bus from Hereford–Woolhope service

From Ross-on-Wye to How Caple the path is fairly level through farmland, but can be muddy in wet weather, particularly close to settlements. A short section of old railway track bed is followed between Ross-on-Wye and Hole-in-the-Wall, and a section of narrow tarmac lane is followed for just over 3km through Foy towards How Caple. Care should be exercised on this section as both vehicles and bicycles use it. How Caple to Fownhope is a mixture of farmland and woodland with some moderate climbs. This stage is not barrier free and therefore not suitable for mobility scooters.

Follow the riverbank upstream from the Hope and Anchor towards the rowing club entrance.

The path leaves the riverbank and passes around the **rowing club buildings**, crossing two small bridges before emerging once more on the riverbank. Bear right to follow the riverbank upstream. Passing beneath the **A40 road bridge**, continue to follow the riverbank. After about 500m turn right and then left (SO 591 255) on to the old track bed of the Gloucester, Ross-on-Wye, Hereford Railway. This line was a victim of the Beeching Report in the 1960s and closed in 1964. ▶ At a crossroads of farm tracks continue for a further 100m, then turn right down some steps (SO 587 263) and follow the edge of the field with the hedge on the right until you reach the apex of a wide bend of the river. Turn right on to the track. ▶

About 30m on, the track splits (SO 589 268) the one straight ahead continuing towards **The Cot**.

The railway track bed is a permissive route by agreement with the landowner, for most of the way, avoiding a walk through fields.

Look left here to see the piers of what was Backney rail bridge.

Map continues
on page 70

The three trees on your right are hornbeams, an unusual tree in Herefordshire.

Turn left and follow the field edge with the hedge on your left. When you reach a small pond turn right and follow the path towards a small wood (**Monks Grove**). Keep the wood on your right. At the north end of the wood, the path on the ground deviates from that shown on your map. At the stile on your right, follow the path through the wood, emerging into the field at a metal kissing gate. Follow the hedge ahead of you. ◄

About two thirds of the way along the second field, bear slightly right towards a large oak tree with a gate at its base at the end of the field. Go through the gate and proceed between the hedge and the conifer plantation. Follow the track through the wood, emerging onto a narrow lane adjacent to **Orchard Cottage** (SO 603 281). Turn left and follow the lane to Foy footbridge.

To visit **St Mary's Church**, Foy, cross the bridge and turn left on to the riverbank path which will take you direct to the church. Return by the same route. The name 'Foy' is an Old French name for faith. The original church on the site was dedicated in the time of Edward

Backney
Common

Foy Bridge

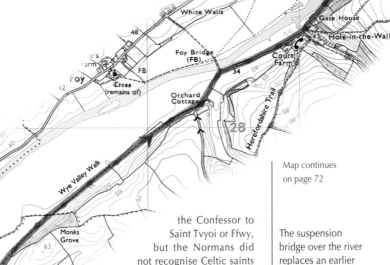

Map continues
on page 72

the Confessor to
Saint Tvyoi or Ffwy,
but the Normans did
not recognise Celtic saints
so they adopted St Foy, and
later, the more typically Norman,
St Mary. ▶

The suspension
bridge over the river
replaces an earlier
bridge washed away
in floods in 1918 and
rebuilt in 1920.

Continue along the road to the quaintly
named **Hole-in-the-Wall**.

This small settlement is believed to have been the
'Thurlstane' mentioned in the Domesday Book meaning
'hole stone', which could easily have become 'Hole in
the Wall'. Note the plaque on the wall of the last building on the right before the cattle grid: 'John Abrahall.
1640'. The Abrahall family was the major landowner in
the area for several generations.

Continue along the road until you reach the second
cattle grid (SO 616 298). Do not cross this, but head off
left to the riverbank and cross the footbridge. Follow the
riverbank until you reach a stream flowing into the Wye
at the end of the field. Bear right and continue to walk
along the field edge with the stream on your left until
you emerge on the road at **How Caple**. Turn left here and
then right beyond the phone box (SO 602 302) to follow

71

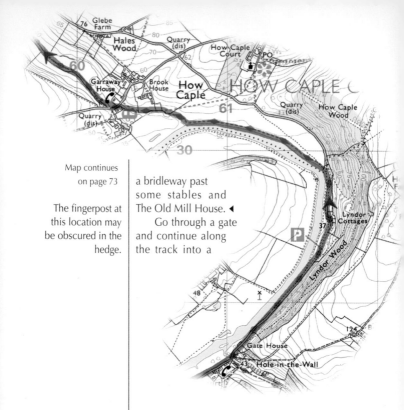

Map continues
on page 73

The fingerpost at
this location may
be obscured in the
hedge.

a bridleway past
some stables and
The Old Mill House. ◄

Go through a gate
and continue along
the track into a

field, following the curving field edge on your left. Near
the end of the narrow field, turn right to cross a footbridge, and go straight up the hill to the right-hand side of
the cottage. At the road, turn left and drop down through

Admire the view from
the field gate back to
Ross, with St Mary's
spire showing against
Chase Hill.

the hamlet of **Totnor**. The redbrick building on your left
after crossing the stream was the blacksmith's forge and
was closed in 1952 when he retired. Keep following the
road uphill, then turn left at the waymarked third trackway on your left (SO 594 315). ◄

At a crossroads of tracks turn right (SO 588 313)
and head up the field edge towards some white houses.
On reaching the road go straight across and follow the
track besides Luiten House, the old stone schoolhouse

building with its bell. This is part of the scattered community of Brockhampton.

Follow this track uphill to reach the road and turn left. ▶ Just beyond the cottage bear right up a track. On reaching a conifer plantation (SO 590 326) again, bear right following through this plantation and then turn right to enter a field where you walk between the defences of yet another Iron Age fort.

There is a small car park with a carved wooden seat giving a good spot to stop and admire the view over the river.

This is a large **hillfort enclosure** with a double set of ramparts and originates from the Iron Age. Archaeological excavations were carried out here in the 1920s and concluded that the site had never been occupied, but more recent excavations have revealed signs of habitation.

Continue to follow the ramparts to a barn on the right. Just after passing the barn, bear downhill and left off the track (SO 595 329) and negotiate a flight of steps down a steep wooded bank. Follow the edge of two fields, skirting around a farm bungalow to the right and cross into the driveway of **Caplor Farm** by the farm shop. Turn right up to the main road.

Turn left along the road then carefully cross over at the first driveway on the right (SO 598 334).

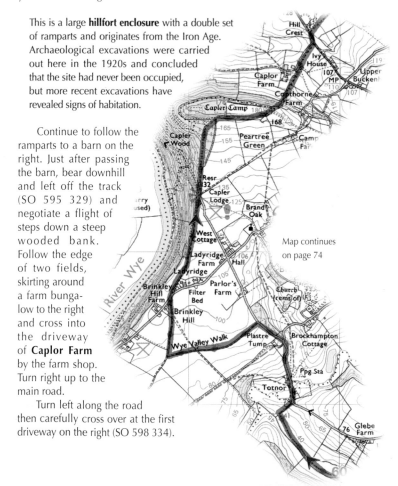

Map continues on page 74

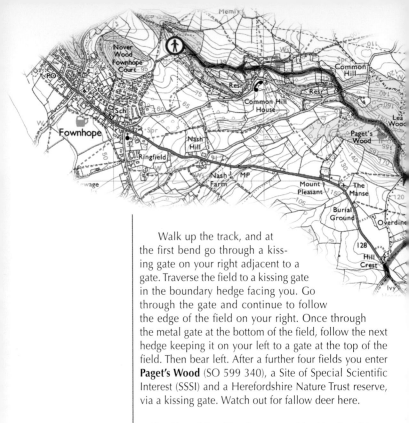

Walk up the track, and at
the first bend go through a kissing gate on your right adjacent to a
gate. Traverse the field to a kissing gate
in the boundary hedge facing you. Go
through the gate and continue to follow
the edge of the field on your right. Once through
the metal gate at the bottom of the field, follow the next
hedge keeping it on your left to a gate at the top of the
field. Then bear left. After a further four fields you enter
Paget's Wood (SO 599 340), a Site of Special Scientific
Interest (SSSI) and a Herefordshire Nature Trust reserve,
via a kissing gate. Watch out for fallow deer here.

> **Paget's** and **Lea Woods**, managed by Herefordshire
> Nature Trust and extending to almost 11ha, are con-
> sidered to be one of the finest ancient, semi-natural,
> broadleaved woodlands in the Wye Valley AONB. The
> name 'Lea' (meaning forest or wood) indicates possi-
> ble Anglo-Saxon origins, and the flora contains a large
> number of ancient woodland indicator species.

At the next junction of paths turn left. Just before
you leave the wood a pair of limekilns dating from at
least 1833 can be seen on your right. Follow the fence
up to the road (SO 595 345), cross over and continue up
the driveway opposite. Take the left fork and at the top

of the slope turn right over a stile, and then left along the ridge path.

The many depressions and hollows alongside the path are disused limestone quarries. After a short distance you pass a seat with a good view of the Wye Valley and drop down through a meadow.

This is another small **nature reserve**, rich in wildflowers and butterflies during the summer months. The Marbled White butterfly is of particular interest because it is uncommon in Herefordshire.

Follow the path down to a crossroads of paths and tracks. At the crossroads continue straight ahead, uphill. Shortly, as you emerge into the open, there is a good view of the west side of Haugh Wood – one of the largest blocks of woodland in Herefordshire – to the right. The ridge top is soon reached. The village of Fownhope and the River Wye can be glimpsed through the trees to the left here.

This is **Common Hill**, one of several limestone ridges making up the Woolhope Dome (an outcrop of Silurian rocks around the village of Woolhope). The area was heavily quarried in the 18th and 19th century and many of the cottages would have been built for the

Limestone flora on North Meadow, Common Hill (Herefordshire Nature Trust)

75

quarry workers. Some interesting limestone flora can be seen during spring and summer, including several species of orchid.

Where a path drops off to your left continue straight on, staying on the high ground, and then go downhill past the next cottage. On reaching the road, cross over and go down the track opposite. However, if you wish to visit the village of **Fownhope** turn left down this road.

FOWNHOPE

The attractive village centre is reached in just under a kilometre. Amenities include shops, a post office, two inns and B&B opportunities. There is an attractive Norman church, with stocks outside, and the village remains one of the few to celebrate Oak Apple Day each May.

Oak Apple Day (or Royal Oak Day) was a public holiday celebrated in England on 29 May to commemorate the restoration of the English monarchy in May 1660, when Charles II returned from exile. Although declared by Parliament as a public holiday, Oak Apple Day was formally abolished in 1859. The wearing of 'oak apples', an abnormal growth or gall formed by the action of a parasitic wasp, commemorates King Charles hiding in an oak tree after the Battle of Worcester in September 1651 to escape the pursuing Parliamentarian soldiers.

Oak Apple Day at Fownhope – Heart of Oak Walk (Kevin Gough)

STAGE 7
Fownhope to Hereford

Start	Fownhope, 700m from village centre, SO 581 351
Finish	Wye Bridge, Hereford, SO 508 395
Distance	11km (6¾ miles)
Time	4hr
Height gain	59m (194ft)
Terrain	Mostly level riverside and field-edge paths, urban routes through Hereford
OS map	Explorer 189 Hereford & Ross-on-Wye
Refreshments	Pubs in Mordiford and Hampton Bishop
Public toilets	None between Fownhope and Hereford
Public transport	On limited days Fownhope can be reached by bus on Hereford–Woolhope service

After a hilly stretch from Fownhope to Mordiford the route is fairly level following the flood plain of the Wye into Hereford. This stage begins with a hilly stretch skirting ancient woodland between Fownhope and Mordiford. The route then levels out, following the flood plain of the Wye. On reaching the outskirts of the city of Hereford the rural tranquillity is replaced temporarily with the buzz of city life.

On reaching the road (SO 581 351) cross over and go down the track opposite. After leaving the road again, the route descends the trackway for a short way, then turns right. After a few more steps go left through the right-hand one of three gates marked as a bridleway. Continue along the edge of the fence and then straight across the open field to a stile. Follow the left-hand side of the hedge opposite you.

Once through the next gate, follow a well-defined track towards a large field oak. The Wye Valley Walk continues through a gate at the end of this field, and straight on down the driveway ahead. Pass through the farmyard and after a few yards turn left along the road (SO 577 368). A little way along there are the remnants of some lovely old orchards, bedecked with mistletoe.

You will pass two cottages on the right. After 90m take the driveway to the right, and then the footpath to the right after a short way.

This area is known as **Bagpiper's Tump**, a strange name to be found in Herefordshire, but during the English Civil War Scottish soldiers of the Parliamentarian army camped here. As pipers are prone to do they probably practised, and the name stuck. 'Tump' refers to a small hill.

After entering the orchard bear left and follow the hedgerow. Cross the stile and continue to the farm buildings. Bear right around these. As you enter the farmyard there is a mill on the left with an intact wheel.

You are entering the village of **Mordiford** (SO 571 373), with the Moon Inn on your right (WVW Passport Stamping Station).

THE LEGENDS OF MORDIFORD

Mordiford developed at the site of an ancient ford over the River Lugg, though this is now crossed by a nine-arched bridge constructed in the 16th century, the oldest road bridge in Herefordshire. Local folklore tells of a fearsome dragon that terrorised the village and was eventually slain by a condemned man, promised his freedom in return. He had himself shut up in a barrel and placed by the river where the dragon was known to drink. He shot the dragon from the bunghole of the barrel, but unfortunately its deadly breath entered the barrel by the same hole and killed him. The alternative story (which bears a bit more credibility) is that Mordred, the younger son of a local king, set himself up in business at a river crossing over the River Lugg and exacted tolls from travellers. He surrounded himself with a gang of ruthless thugs, so that the locals were terrorised by him and hated him. The crossing became known as 'Mordred's Ford', hence Mordiford. The dragon? Mordred's standard carried the symbol of a green dragon and thus was born a subtle means of telling the story of Mordred's deeds in front of a fire on a dark night. Needless to say Mordred came to a sticky end!

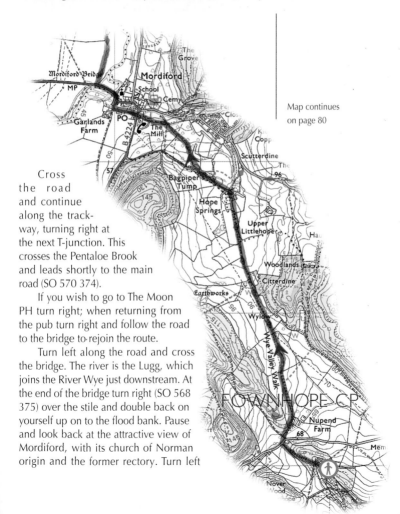

Map continues on page 80

Cross the road and continue along the track-way, turning right at the next T-junction. This crosses the Pentaloe Brook and leads shortly to the main road (SO 570 374).

If you wish to go to The Moon PH turn right; when returning from the pub turn right and follow the road to the bridge to rejoin the route.

Turn left along the road and cross the bridge. The river is the Lugg, which joins the River Wye just downstream. At the end of the bridge turn right (SO 568 375) over the stile and double back on yourself up on to the flood bank. Pause and look back at the attractive view of Mordiford, with its church of Norman origin and the former rectory. Turn left

River Wye at Hampton Bishop (Michael Mable)

and continue along the bank for approximately 1.2km, passing several gates.

Sufton, the home of the Hereford family, Lords of the Manor since the 12th century, stands prominently off to the right.

When you reach a stock-holding pen turn left along

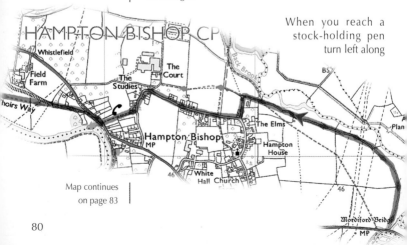

Map continues on page 83

80

the lane, and then right at the next junction (SO 559 382). This is the village of **Hampton Bishop**. ▶

Follow Rectory Road to the right for about 800m. Keep going until you reach a fingerpost next to a brick garden wall. Turn right off the road (SO 552 382). Enter the field and head straight across to a stile on the edge of the road. The route goes straight on here. If refreshments are required, the Bunch of Carrots PH lies 140m down the road to the left.

Cross over the road here and up the steps onto the flood bank (SO 549 382). Turn immediately right through a kissing gate and continue along the flood bank. Just beyond the next kissing gate, veer off left and down to the footbridge and from here across the field to the riverbank. Turn right through a kissing gate and follow the riverbank for several fields. The hill on the opposite bank is Dinedor, one of a number in the area to be capped with Iron Age forts.

Eventually the route leads away from the river to a further kissing gate, situated in the corner of the field. Turn right from here. Pass a housing estate on your left

If you wish to visit the interesting picturesque Norman church of St Andrew with its unusual ground plan and medieval roof timbers, go left at this point.

The old Wye Bridge, Hereford (Michael Mable)

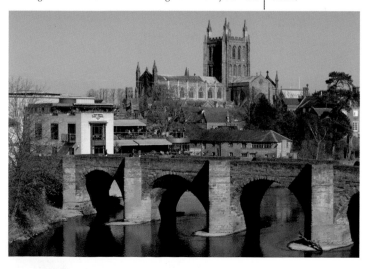

and go through
three more kissing gates to meet the road into
Hereford (SO 535 391). Cross over the road and turn left,
continuing along the road.

After you pass beneath a railway bridge, take the next
left into Park Street (SO 519 394). At the end of this road
turn right and first left into Vicarage Road. At the end of

Hereford
(Michael Mable)

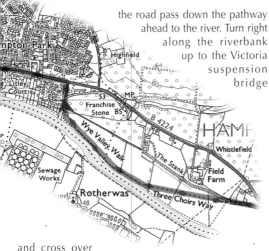

the road pass down the pathway
ahead to the river. Turn right
along the riverbank
up to the Victoria
suspension
bridge

and cross over
the river into Bishops
Meadow. Turn right and follow the riverbank, with its
view of the cathedral, up to the old six-arched **Wye
Bridge**. As you approach the bridge notice the difference
in the shape of the arches. Which is the one rebuilt after
being blown up during the English Civil War?

HEREFORD

The city grew up around an ancient river crossing, explaining its name,
which means the 'ford of the army' in Anglo-Saxon English. Sites of interest
include the cathedral dating from 1079, and Mappa Mundi, a 13th-century
world map, showing Jerusalem as the centre of the world, now housed in
a purpose-built building along with a medieval chained library. Bulmers,
the cider maker, has its factory and headquarters in Hereford, and a cider
museum is open to the public. There is a Waterworks Museum just off
the Wye Valley Walk at Broomy Hill, based on a Victorian water-pump-
ing station. The well-established Three Choirs Festival rotates annually
between Hereford and the cities of Worcester and Gloucester. As would be
expected of a city, Hereford has all the facilities walkers require, including
a railway station.

STAGE 8
Hereford to Byford

Start	Wye Bridge, Hereford, SO 508 395
Finish	Byford church, SO 397 429
Distance	15.6km (9¾ miles)
Time	3hr 45min
Height gain	150m (490ft)
Terrain	Riverside paths, field edges and long stretch of fairly quiet road; A438 crossed twice
OS maps	Explorers 189 Hereford & Ross-on-Wye, 202 Leominster & Bromyard, 201 Knighton & Presteigne
Refreshments	Supermarket close to start with toilets and refreshments available until quite late; no other facilities on or close to this stage
Public toilets	None on route
Public transport	Limited bus service to Byford from Hereford-to-Breinton route

Starting in Hereford the route follows the riverbank to Breinton where there is a slight climb to a car park. From then on the path generally follows surfaced roads, headland field paths and a bridleway. There are several stiles and one very narrow kissing gate, and a major road which has to be negotiated twice.

Cross over the road on reaching the 15th-century Wye Bridge, remaining on the same side of the river. The blue plaque on the wall of the Saracen's Head PH gives a brief history of the bridge, which was one of the main entrances to the ancient city of Hereford.

Shortly you pass under the new road bridge. Continue to the **disused railway bridge** at Hunderton. Climb the steps to the left and cross over the bridge descending to the opposite bank. Continue along the riverbank. A right-hand

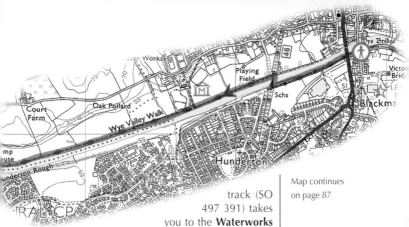

track (SO 497 391) takes you to the **Waterworks Museum**. ▶

The path soon emerges into open countryside again, and follows the riverbank through several fields with **Belmont golf course** and Belmont Abbey on the opposite bank.

Where the path meets a wooded bank, at a wooden kissing gate and a Wye Valley Walk information board (SO 474 392), you enter **Breinton Common**. This 6ha common is owned and managed by the National Trust.

Map continues on page 87

This section from Hereford to Breinton is a popular riverside stroll from the city.

Breinton church (Michael Mable)

85

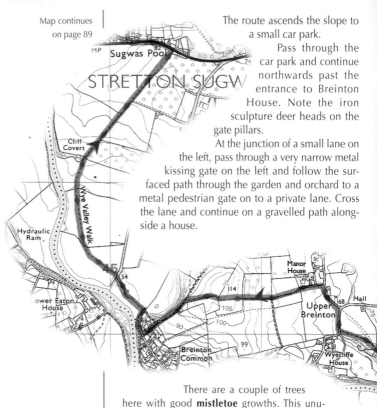

Map continues
on page 89

The route ascends the slope to a small car park.

Pass through the car park and continue northwards past the entrance to Breinton House. Note the iron sculpture deer heads on the gate pillars.

At the junction of a small lane on the left, pass through a very narrow metal kissing gate on the left and follow the surfaced path through the garden and orchard to a metal pedestrian gate on to a private lane. Cross the lane and continue on a gravelled path alongside a house.

There are a couple of trees here with good **mistletoe** growths. This unusual hemi-parasitic plant celebrated in folklore is now quite rare nationally, but is still common in Herefordshire.

Although the path at the hilltop is only 107m high, it affords good views back into Hereford City and forward to the Welsh hills, giving an idea of the delights to come.

Turn left into an arable field through a wooden kissing gate, keeping to the left-hand side of the field, and go on through a further field. On reaching the road (SO 465 400) descend the flight of steps and turn right. After about 150m a road junction is reached. Turn left towards 'Sugwas and Swainshill'. Turn left into the bridleway on the left just after Manor Cottages (SO 464 403). Follow the bridleway. ◄

SIR EDWARD ELGAR

At the top of the bank are earthworks, thought to be the remains of a medieval moated manor house built during the 12th century. Behind this lies Breinton church. This is one of the many sites in the area with connections to the English composer Sir Edward Elgar, as his friend, Canon Charles Vincent Gorton of Manchester Cathedral, is buried in the churchyard. Gorton commissioned Elgar to adjudicate at the Morecambe Music Festival and they became close friends. The lychgate is of interest as this was the original entrance to the graveyard, but was replaced by a more convenient entrance from the north thereby avoiding the often waterlogged approach over the common.

On reaching the top of the hill go through the right-hand gate and follow the hedge around to the left through the bridlegate and down the track between houses to the road. There is a view of the river on the way. Turn right to descend the escarpment. On the right is a cottage with memorials carved into the beams.

At the next bend to the right go left over a stile (SO 450 403) and continue straight ahead to the corner of the hedge opposite. There is a double stile just to the left of the corner: cross it and head off in an 11 o'clock direction. As you clear the rise you should see the next stile in the hedge ahead of you. From here head for the gateway with an adjacent stile in the next field, between a wood and orchard (SO 448 411).

Once over the stile keep to the right-hand edge of the next two fields until you reach the main road. Cross the road here and turn left towards the old Kite's Nest Inn, which is now an Indian restaurant.

RED KITES

The references to 'kite's nest' in the name of farms, public houses and woods are pointers to the once common sight of red kites in England and Wales. Due to persecution by Victorian gamekeepers and changes in urban environmental health the numbers of red kite in Britain fell to just two pairs in the Welsh hills in the 1930s. Legal protection and the physical protection

by the RSPB along with many dedicated volunteers has seen numbers rise over the last 30 years, so that red kites are now a fairly common sight especially in Mid Wales and various areas of England where there have been reintroduction schemes, such as in the Chiltern Hills near High Wycombe.

At the end of the footway, bear right down a metalled road which develops into a wide lane between houses. Skirt around to the right of the last house and enter the field. From here, follow the hedge line straight ahead until you reach the road. At the road turn right.

As you step on to the road you are standing on a Roman road which once linked the crossing of the River Wye with the settlement of **Magna Castra**. (On the OS Map is it spelt 'Magnis' but this is now deemed to be a modern misspelling.) ◄ After rejoining the road continue on past

The modern road northwards deviates from the Roman road.

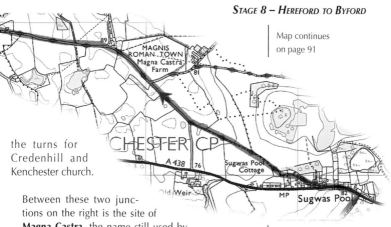

Map continues
on page 91

the turns for Credenhill and Kenchester church.

Between these two junctions on the right is the site of **Magna Castra**, the name still used by the farm to the east. This was a walled urban settlement believed to have been the home of the settled Dobunni, the local British tribal group. Roads passed through the town from all points of the compass, so it is obvious that this was an important junction at one time, possibly concerned with trade from the Cheshire salt mines.

Remaining on the road, you pass through the village of **Bishopstone**, eventually to reach a crossroads. Cross over, following the sign to Garnons. You are now on a Roman road which went westwards from Magna

OFFA'S DYKE

After about 850m, where the road passes between woodland on the hill to the right and below to the left (SO 405 434), you cross the line of Offa's Dyke. This earthwork of a bank and ditch is believed to have been constructed on the orders of King Offa, who was king of the English kingdom of Mercia from AD757 to 796. This construction would have crossed the Roman road at this point, being much later in date, but there is no evidence that the road was built over, so it appears the dyke was not continuous at this point. It is interesting to speculate that if the dyke was meant to be a political boundary, Wales and the Welsh must have covered a very large part of what is now Herefordshire at that time.

89

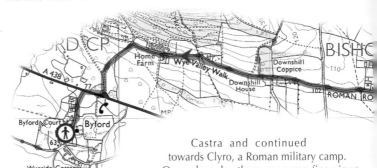

Castra and continued towards Clyro, a Roman military camp.

On a clear day there are some fine views across towards the Black Mountains from this road. Some impressive parkland trees start to appear beyond the entrance to the Garnons Estate, home of the Cotterell family since 1832.

Bear left at the end of the road and right on to the main road at the Gate House. Caution is needed here, as this is a busy section. Take the first road left signed **Byford** (SO 397 431).

The Wye at Hereford

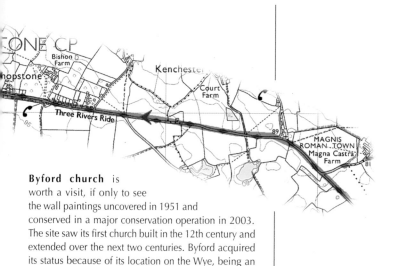

Byford church is
worth a visit, if only to see
the wall paintings uncovered in 1951 and
conserved in a major conservation operation in 2003.
The site saw its first church built in the 12th century and
extended over the next two centuries. Byford acquired
its status because of its location on the Wye, being an
important ferry and fording site.

Byford has no shops or accommodation.

91

STAGE 9

Byford to Bredwardine

Start	Byford church, SO 397 429
Finish	Red Lion Hotel, Bredwardine, SO 331 444
Distance	7.7km (4¾ miles)
Time	2hr
Height gain	88m (289ft)
Terrain	Mainly field paths and farm tracks through orchards; about a mile of road walking on quiet lanes at end
OS map	Explorer 201 Knighton & Presteigne
Refreshments	None on route
Public toilets	None on route
Public transport	None between Byford and Bredwardine; bus service between Hereford and Bredwardine (check timetables)

This stage is an easy walk through apple orchards and fields, passing a small but interesting church and a mile-long avenue of trees, crossing the Wye at Bredwardine Bridge and passing historic Bredwardine church before ending at the Red Lion Hotel.

From Byford church continue down the lane to a junction with an unsurfaced bridleway on the right (SO 396 428). Follow this bridleway past the entrance to a farm.

On your right you will see some old apple trees. The bridleway is well defined along the headland and has some fine large oak trees. At the far end of a group of poplars the track makes a dogleg, right then left, with the next

Apple blossom in Bulmers' orchard

hedge on your right. At this point you will see a church and farm buildings on the left. This is Preston Court, on the other side of the river.

Keep to the side of the field and cross over a stream into an extensive cider apple orchard owned by Bulmers of Hereford. A noticeboard welcomes walkers and explains the varieties planted and the uses they are put to.

At the riverbank turn right and follow the edge of the orchard until you see a small church on the left. This is St Mary's at **Monnington**.

As you approach Monnington church, turn left (SO 374 433), crossing what was once a dam holding back the stream to form a pond. On reaching the churchyard turn immediately right and skirt the graves to the lychgate. ▶

Note the wide oak 'seat', used for resting coffins on to await the arrival of the vicar.

Map continues on page 97

ST MARY'S CHURCH

If you do not take time to have a look in the church, you miss a little gem of history. St Mary's of Monnington on Wye is an unusual church, as it has no road access and is surrounded by water on three sides. It is still lit by oil lamps as there is no electricity connection. The earliest church was built in the 13th century but rebuilt in 1679 by Uvedfale Tomkins of Monnington Court, which adjoins the church.

James Tomkins, grandfather of Uvedfale, was a staunch supporter of the king during the English Civil War and was hung in 1643 by the Parliamentarians for raising a troop of soldiers for the king's cause. Such was the family's support for the king that a splendid Royal Coat of Arms was erected in the church to celebrate the Restoration of Charles II.

Follow the path ahead with the stream on your right. When you reach the metalled driveway go left, then curve right around the front of the redbrick house to enter Monnington Walk.

*Monnington Walk
(Michael Mable)*

Monnington Walk is a mile-long avenue of Scots pine and yew trees planted in 1623 by James Tomkins of

Monnington Court to celebrate his election as Member of Parliament for Leominster. It is unlikely that any of the original trees other than some of the yews survive, although one or two of the Scots pines are of considerable age. Failures or casualties continue to be replaced by the present owners.

Walk the length of Monnington Walk, which is designated as a public bridleway, and admire the views between the trees. ▶

Bear right through a gate and immediately left to follow the side of the wood. At the end of the second field (SO 354 444) go left through the bridlegate to re-enter the wood.

You are at the beginning of **Brobury Scar** here, where the river has cut deep into the sandstone to create a cliff-like bluff. Notice the gnarled old chestnut trees alongside the path too.

Continue along the main path at the edge of the wood but take time to view the 92m drop to the river below, and

Note on the right just before you reach the western end a headstone over the grave of 'Springervale Pecora. 1971–1996. Great show horse. Lifter of spirit.'

Brobury Scar (Michael Mable)

across to Moccas
Park in the distance; the
park was designed by Capability Brown, one
of Britain's greatest landscape architects.

The large hill ahead is Merbach Hill. The next stage of the Walk will take you over its summit.

On meeting the road (SO 351 445) turn left. ◄

On reaching the next junction, follow the lane to the right. When a crossroads is reached turn left and follow the road down to Bredwardine Bridge.

REV FRANCIS KILVERT

Bredwardine Church, dedicated to St Andrew, is of Norman origin but was considerably altered in 1875. Like so many other Norman church sites it is probable there was originally a Celtic Christian church here.

As you enter the churchyard a memorial seat to the Rev Francis Kilvert under the huge yew tree commemorates the association of this famous diarist with St Andrews. Kilvert, originally from Wiltshire, was ordained a priest in Bristol in 1864 and held various posts until being appointed to St Andrews in 1877. Throughout his life he kept a diary recording the day-to-day events of life as he saw them. His diaries tell of a way of life on the Welsh Border country now long gone, but the detail gives an accurate picture recorded nowhere else. Today the Kilvert Society continues to keep his name and his diaries alive in the area Kilvert loved, lived in and sadly, at the very young age of 38, died. His grave is a marble cross on the north side of the church.

Bredwardine Bridge replaced a ferry over the Wye and is unusual in being almost completely constructed of bricks. Its six arches provide an attractive foreground for a very lovely section of the River Wye. Originally built as a toll road it was eventually taken over by Herefordshire County Council and extensive repairs carried out in 1921. It is recorded that on 10 February 1795 the greatest

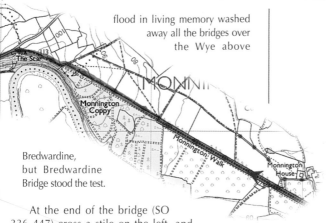

flood in living memory washed away all the bridges over the Wye above Bredwardine, but Bredwardine Bridge stood the test.

At the end of the bridge (SO 336 447) cross a stile on the left, and follow the riverside path to a gated footbridge. Follow the path uphill towards Bredwardine church and Old Vicarage, crossing a stile (SO 334 445) on to the access road to the Old Vicarage. Continue along this track to Bredwardine church on the left.

From the church continue down the drive along the avenue of beech trees. Turn left at the road junction.

At the next crossroads, go straight over to the Red Lion Hotel, the only establishment in Bredwardine offering accommodation and refreshments.

*Bredwardine Bridge
(Michael Mable)*

STAGE 10
Bredwardine to Hay-on-Wye

Start	Red Lion Hotel, Bredwardine, SO 331 444
Finish	Wye Bridge, Hay-on-Wye, SO 228 425
Distance	13.6km (8½ miles)
Time	4hr 30min
Height gain	426m (1396ft)
Terrain	Very steep initial climb, then gradual ascent through pasture and woodlands to Merbach Hill; steep descent then undulating route with no more steep gradients
OS map	Explorer 201 Knighton & Presteigne
Refreshments	None on route; in Hay-on-Wye
Public toilets	None on route; in Hay-on-Wye by clock tower
Public transport	Brecon-to-Hereford bus services pass through Hay-on-Wye; service between Hereford and Bredwardine

This stage starts with a steep climb out of Bredwardine but the views gained are well worth the effort. Merbach Hill (318m) gives the first views of the Welsh Hills but also of the Malverns. This was the land of the Marcher Lords of Norman times and the route passes historic remains, including a motte-and-bailey castle and the site of a priory. From more recent times the route follows drovers' trails and the track of an old railway. There are many stiles on this stage.

From the Red Lion Hotel at Bredwardine turn left by the Wye Valley Walk information board and walk uphill on the surfaced public road. This is a very steep start but at the entrance to Cwm Farm on the left there is an opportunity to have a rest and look back over the way you have come, down to Bredwardine Bridge and the River Wye. After just under 600m turn right on to a marked bridleway, ignoring the footpath stile in the corner of the field. Follow the track past a cottage until a field gate is reached, pass through and turn immediately left with a stream on your left. Follow the stream uphill and pass through a wooden gate. Turn half-right and continue uphill through the field until the hill flattens out. Continue ahead downhill towards a metal gate on a stoned track ahead. The views from this hill – although you are not at the highest point – are well worth the effort of getting there: you are looking north over the Herefordshire Plain with the River Wye gliding like a silver thread through the middle foreground.

Continue along the track marked 'Woolla' through woodland. As you approach the farm the path turns half-left (SO 317 448) and climbs through the wood to a wooden gate to emerge on to a stoned track overlooking the farm with extensive views to the north. ▶

Continue through a further three fields before finally reaching the open expanse of Merbach Common. Go right over the stile here and then left after 23m. This is a permissive route on to Merbach Common and can be used by walkers. The Public Right of Way is through the metal gate straight ahead as you enter the third field.

The route bears right just before the summit of **Merbach Hill**. ▶

At a three-way junction not marked on your map (SO 304 447) take the right fork and the path starts to descend the north side of Merbach Hill, becoming increasingly steep and narrow until a junction is reached with the Herefordshire Trail joining from

Note that this is a permissive route, so there is a divergence between your OS Map and what is on the ground.

A short detour to the left soon leads to the summit cairn. It is claimed 11 counties may be seen from here on a clear day.

Map continues on page 103

Low sun near Merbach (Michael Mable)

the left. The two routes now share the same paths for some time. Continue downhill, passing an information board and exiting Merbach Common by a gate where the ground can be very muddy in wet weather. Continue downhill on an enclosed track which shows signs of old stone surfacing, bearing left with the track to eventually reach a surfaced public road.

Turn right and follow the road to some farm buildings. Go straight ahead at the corner, keeping the farm buildings on your left (SO 290 447), and follow this grass track to the B4352. Turn left here (SO 291 452). ▸

Take care on the next section as there are bends and no footway.

MERBACH COMMON

Once an important grazing area for local farms, Merbach Common is now a nature reserve under the management of the Herefordshire Nature Trust. The highest point on the common is 318m and was once quarried. Managed now for the diversity of wildlife, with dormice and several species of butterflies and birds, it is (like all registered commons in England and Wales), 'Open Access' status for walking under the Countryside and Rights of Way Act 2000.

The Wye Valley Walk follows a registered public bridleway. It has been suggested that this route may have been used by Welsh drovers to bring cattle and other livestock to the markets of the Midlands and London until the coming of the railways. This might account for the signs of surfacing along the path, which was obviously designed for heavier usage than by walkers or even horses.

After an ornate set of gates with shields emblazoned with a 'Fleur de Lys', turn right on a marked bridleway (SO 288 452). At the end of the grounds of the house turn left over a stile into the field and follow the field edge, emerging onto the road again opposite **Old Castleton**. Turn right here and continue for just over 820m past Lower Castleton, passing the site of a large **motte & bailey castle** on your right.

The origin of this castle is unknown, but it is probably one of many fortifications erected by the **Norman Marcher Lords** to control crossings on the Wye. It is on private property so do not enter the field. 'Marcher', meaning border, originated from an Old Norman term referring to the border between Normandy and Brittany, and was transferred by them to the Welsh border country.

Just before the top of the hill turn right through the gateway (SO 278 456) and head across the field, slightly down the slope, and through a plantation of trees. Cross the bottom of the next field. Note the evidence of stone surfacing along this track which leads directly to an important river crossing at Whitney-on-Wye.

Wildfowl often gather on this stretch of river during the winter months. Wigeon, teal and goosander sometimes join the regular mallard and mute swans, and migratory Bewick's swans may occasionally be seen. Their musical trumpeting calls and yellow-and-black bills distinguish them from their resident cousins.

At the end of the wood pass into pastureland. It is at this point the Herefordshire Trail and the Wye Valley Walk part company (SO 272 460): the Herefordshire Trail continues straight ahead to cross the River Wye at

Whitney-on-Wye, while the Wye Valley Walk bears half-

Map continues on page 107

left on a permissive path, uphill to the edge of woodland, skirts the wood, crosses two stiles and emerges into a field with a level track on your left. You are now on the former track bed of the Golden Valley Railway.

From the stile at the top of the field there are good views over the meandering river towards Whitney Bridge (toll). The area below is known as **Locksters Pool**, one of several famous salmon pools along this stretch of river.

THE GOLDEN VALLEY RAILWAY

This railway had a short existence. Built as a narrow gauge railway to improve trade and communications in what was then a fairly remote area, the line started from Pontrilas in the south to Dorstone, and then Hay-on-Wye in the north, between 1876 and 1889. It was never a financial success and closed in 1898, to be bought for £9000 by the Great Western Railway who reopened the route in 1901. Eventually, due to the increase in road transport, it succumbed and the last train to Hay-on-Wye ran in 1949. The only traces remaining today are the bits of track bed and the occasional stone road bridge or level crossing.

Just before you reach an old railway bridge, turn left through a gate and left along the road. Continue uphill passing **The Farm** on your right. At the second property on the right, do not be distracted by the sculptures in the garden, and turn left opposite the entrance over a stile into a field (SO 261 457) and continue through a further two fields to emerge on Clifford Common, owned by the parish. Continue straight ahead over the common to the higher public road.

Turn right and follow this to the Calvanistic Methodist Chapel, now defunct. Opposite the chapel, turn left off the road into another small grass field and re-emerge on to the

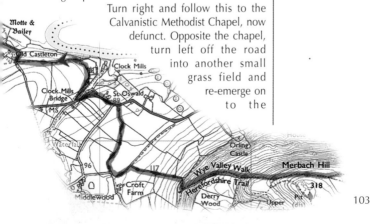

public road once more. Turn left and walk downhill to a three-way junction with a row of houses; St Mary's Church is to the right. The Wye Valley Walk continues straight ahead, through a gate at the extreme left of the houses. This is a very narrow path leading to a stile into a field. Turn half-right and follow the path to the next stile ahead. Cross the stile and the path is straight ahead, downhill. At this point the Welsh hills come into view, and a good marker for the path is to keep a very large lime tree on the left and the Brecon Beacons to the right: the path is between them. At the cattle grid and gate turn left on to the public road.

Walk downhill and at the second gateway, just beyond an ancient oak which is now sadly collapsed but still hanging on to life, turn right into the field.

THE PRIORY

The large farm opposite is Priory Farm, one of the principal farms of the area. In 1129–30 in the reign of Henry I, a local lord, Simon Fitz Richard granted land for the Cluniac Order to establish a cell for monks, which later became a priory. The order originated in Cluny in Burgundy and became the most important monastic order in Europe for a time. Eventually 22 Cluniac monks left the order and established the Cistercian Order. At the Dissolution of the Monasteries by Henry VIII in 1536, the land and buildings were taken over by the Crown and sold off to various loyal families. The farm eventually became the property of Benjamin Haigh Allen in the mid-1800s, who was the High Sheriff of Herefordshire. By this time the farmhouse was a very substantial building, probably built from the stone of the priory and further improved in Georgian style. The Rev Robert Francis Kilvert, the famous diarist, then curate at Clyro, records a visit to The Priory on 12 July 1870 with friends to witness the eclipse of the moon in the company of the Allen family.

The path across the golf course is well marked with posts, but take care and be wary of golfers who may be hitting balls across the footpath.

The path follows an attractive dingle until you reach a ford and footbridge over Hardwicke Brook. Follow the right-hand side of the hedge, veering off to the right just before the end of the field and cross the stile on to **Summerhill Golf Course**. ◄

At the south end of the course, cross a stile into an enclosed path and continue into the field at a second

*Hardwicke Brook
(Michael Mable)*

stile. Follow the headland of the field straight ahead to a third stile and gate, then a series of gates follows, crossing an old avenue of trees which once led to The Moor, an old mansion.

The tower visible on the left is one of the few remaining features of **The Moor**. The main house is now gone, but a walled garden and fishponds remain.

HAY-ON-WYE

Hay-on-Wye is billed as the 'bookshop capital of the world', and a short walk around the town will help to convince you that this is the case. It also has a plethora of cafés, hotels, B&B establishments and restaurants to cater for most needs. There are shops, banks, a post office and a TIC. Public transport is available, but times are variable and should be checked beforehand.

Hay-on-Wye with its castle is now clearly visible ahead. After a further three stiles the road is reached. Turn right, and on the next bend in the road take the footpath

Bookshop at Hay-on-Wye (Michael Mable)

off to the left behind the bench. Drop down and through the Scudamore Dingle, a deepwater course which in storm conditions must see a huge flow of water coming straight from the hills. Once in the field head for the white gabled house slightly to the right.

Descend to the Dulas Brook, marking the boundary with England and Wales, and enter the Brecon Beacons National Park. Having crossed the Dulas Brook from Herefordshire take the path across Black Lion Green, with the cottages to the right, to the top of the bank where you enter Black Lion

Lane. From here there is a choice: either turn left into Hay, or turn right to stay on the Wye Valley Walk, which skirts the town.

Keeping to the walk, at the end of the lane go through the wicket gate and follow the enclosed path to Newport Street (B4350). Here, again, you can turn left along the road to explore Hay, or keep on the Walk by taking Wyeford Road opposite to the riverside path. On reaching the river turn left along

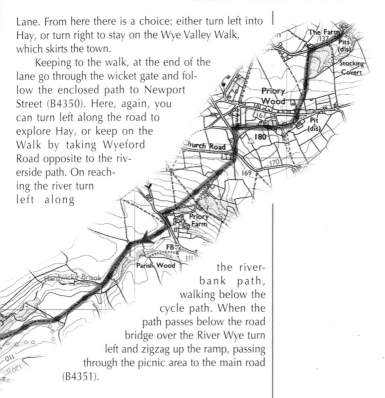

the riverbank path, walking below the cycle path. When the path passes below the road bridge over the River Wye turn left and zigzag up the ramp, passing through the picnic area to the main road (B4351).

STAGE 11

Hay-on-Wye to Glasbury

Start	Wye Bridge, Hay-on-Wye, SO 228 425
Finish	Glasbury Bridge, SO 178 392
Distance	7.7km (4¾ miles); alternative route (nr Llowes) 8.1km (5 miles)
Time	2hr 20min (alternative route 2hr 50min)
Height gain	47m (155ft) from Llowes to Brynyrhydd Farm, otherwise negligible; alternative route 177m (581ft)
Terrain	Mostly riverbank path; alternative route steep climb then more gradual descent into Llowes, followed by short but steep climb and steep descent on road to A438
OS map	Explorer OL13 Brecon Beacons National Park, or Explorer 201 Knighton & Presteigne and Explorer 188 Builth Wells
Refreshments	Pub at Llowes (variable opening); café and service station/shop at Glasbury on south side of bridge; pub in Glasbury at start of Stage 12
Public toilets	Hay-on-Wye by clock tower and Glasbury by bridge
Public transport	Hereford-to-Brecon bus stops at Glasbury, Clyro and Hay-on-Wye

Back in Wales on this stage for some fairly easy river valley walking, following mainly field-edge paths with some sections on main road verges and a little surfaced lane walking. The alternative route near Llowes does involve some climbing, but the stunning views of the Black Mountains and Brecon Beacons make it well worth it. There are a few stiles on this stage.

Leave Hay-on-Wye by crossing the road bridge over the Wye towards Clyro, keeping to the right-hand footway. The Wye Valley Walk briefly shares the pavement here with the Offa's Dyke Path National Trail that was last encountered in Monmouth. The National Trail turns off to

Hay Castle (Michael Mable)

the right at the end of the bridge, but for the Wye Valley Walk continue on the pavement uphill to where the road starts to bend right. On the opposite side of the road is a kissing gate (SO 225 428). Take care and cross the road to this gate. Look back at the view of Hay-on-Wye with the castle still dominating the town, but look forward and in the distance the Brecon Beacons dominate the skyline.

Keep straight on with the hedge on your right to a gate into woodland. The river is below you, and to your right as you descend the bank is a huge stone retaining wall for the garden of **Wyecliff** above. Follow the path down, crossing a bridge and emerging on to a stoned track. Turn left and follow the path to the right, keeping a garden hedge to your left. The path now follows the north bank of the Wye with views to the left towards the Black Mountains and to the right towards Clyro church tower.

KILVERT AND CONAN DOYLE

This is Kilvert Country – the Rev Robert Francis Kilvert was the curate at Clyro from 1865 to 1872 and much of the material in his diaries covers this period (see Stage 9). He delighted in exploring the local landscape and followed many of the country paths that are still in use today. In 1877 Kilvert became vicar of Bredwardine and married in August 1879, but died just weeks later aged 38. He is buried at Bredwardine.

To your right appears Baskerville House Hotel, the former home of the Baskerville family who were friends of Sir Arthur Conan Doyle, who is alleged to have had the idea for his Sherlock Holmes book *The Hound of the Baskervilles* while staying at the house.

The path now continues along the riverbank for 2.4km with large arable fields on your right. Follow the fence edge to avoid riverbank erosion. Towards the end of this riverside section there is a choice of which route to take into Llowes.

For a level and easy walk continue to the end of this riverside section and head right over the field, pass through a kissing gate and turn left. A short path then leads to a lay-by at the edge of the main road (A438). Follow the footway for 800m until you reach the village of Llowes. This section of road is quite busy but visibility is good.

Map continues
on page 113

Approaching Llowes (Michael Mable)

For a steeper walk that provides stunning views of the Wye Valley and the Brecon Beacons (and avoids the roadside walking) turn right on entering the final large field and follow the headland path up to the main road (A438). Cross the road with care and take the footpath that leads diagonally left up across the field. This is quite a climb but the views are worth it! Go through the pedestrian gate at the top of this field and follow the hedge uphill, then cross the field, pass through a gate and follow the path that runs below **Briwnant** and crosses two further fields before joining a track leading down to Llowes.

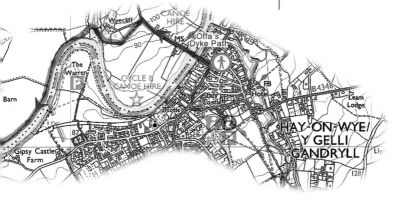

The Wye Valley Walk continues past the church to the next junction with a telephone box and bus shelter, opposite the Seren Bach campsite (SO 192 416). Turn right and follow the road uphill. As an alternative (if visiting St Meilig's Church) pass through the churchyard, visit the church, then continue through the churchyard to the road beyond and join the 'official' route by turning right over the stream.

ST MEILIG'S CHURCH

There has been a church or religious centre here – the site of a Celtic Christian monk's cell or early monastery – for over 1300 years. A monk from Clydesdale in Scotland settled here and soon gathered converts to him and became St Meilig, to whom the church is dedicated. Monks from southern Scotland would have been quite at ease in Wales at that time, as Welsh was the common language. The name 'Llowes' is believed to come from the Celtic monk St Llywes who settled in the area at about the same time as Meilig. The church underwent Victorian 'modernisation' in the 1850s as the old church was still substantially a medieval building. Inside is a Celtic stone cross known as St Meilig's Cross; this originally stood on the Begwn Mountain Common at Croesfeilliog but was brought to the churchyard at Llowes for safety in the 12th century, and re-erected in 1956 inside the church to protect it from the elements. Crosses were used as monastic boundary markers, memorials or simply as focus points for gatherings. Also in the church is a pre-Norman font, which was found being used as a flowerpot in the Rectory garden.

St Meiligs would have been familiar to Francis Kilvert as the rector, Rev Thomas Williams, was a friend and Kilvert visited him regularly. There is a sundial in the churchyard alongside the path dedicated to Kilvert, erected by the Kilvert Society.

The route continues uphill, passing a farm with converted barns on your left to a kissing gate (SO191417). Turn left through the gate, over a stile (with a field gate to the side) and then through another gate. At this gate head uphill at about 1 o'clock to a pedestrian gate, almost hidden in the corner of a wood that is part of Bryn-yr-Hydd Common.

Before you reach this gate, a look back towards Llowes and across the flood plain of the Wye gives good views of the **Black Mountains** to the south. The higher hills (from the left) are Hay Bluff and the curiously named Lord Hereford's Knob or the Twmpa. The wooded hill in the middle foreground is The Allt or yr Allt, a common name in Wales for such a landscape feature.

The path through the wood can be narrow and root-covered, but note the covered well on the right of the path. On reaching a bridleway turn left, and pass through the yard of **Brynyrhydd Farm**.

The route now descends sharply past a red-brick building, **Bryn-yr-Hydd House**, formerly the home of the Beavan family who feature so much in the affairs of Llowes. On the right is

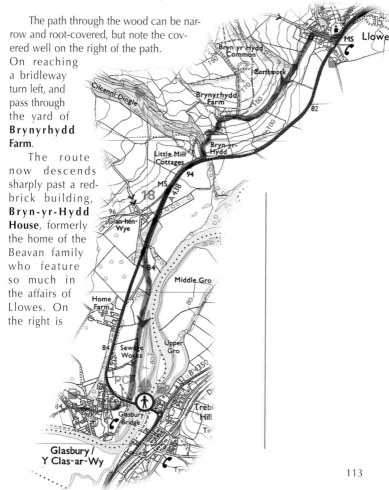

Glasbury / Y Clas-ar-Wy

113

The Wye at Glasbury (Jon Dixon)

Cilcenni Dingle is a 17ha woodland in a deeply incised dingle or valley cut through Devonian sandstone by a stream that feeds into the Wye.

Cilcenni Dingle, a woodland owned and managed by the Woodland Trust with informal access for the public. ◄

Continue downhill to the A438 (SO 183 408). Cross the road and use the grass verge for about 800m until reaching a wooden kissing gate just past the turning for Maesyronnen (SO 179 401). Go through this gate and two more gates crossing what was once the main road, but now a farm track, and aim quarter-right to where the path meets the river edge. Now follow the riverside path through several gates, passing a small water treatment works, until you emerge on to the A438 at **Glasbury Bridge** (SO 178 392). The fields here are dotted with fine oak trees and mistletoe can be seen hanging from a line of poplars bordering the river.

GLASBURY

The village of Glasbury is split by the River Wye. There are toilets adjoining the bridge, and a café and a service station on the opposite side of the bridge. There are accommodation providers and pubs in the village.

STAGE 12

Glasbury to Erwood

Start	Glasbury Bridge, SO 178 392
Finish	Erwood Bridge, SO 089 437
Distance	14km (8¾ miles)
Time	3hr 15min
Height gain	Negligible
Terrain	Mostly tracks and field paths but some road sections (including very short stretch on verge of busy A470)
OS map	Explorer 188 Builth Wells
Refreshments	Cafe and service station/shop south side Glasbury Bridge, pub on route in Glasbury; village shop in Boughrood, pub just over Boughrood Bridge. Pub, café and petrol station/shop, accommodation in Llyswen (short detour)
Public toilets	Glasbury by bridge, Erwood Station Craft Centre (when open)
Public transport	Brecon-to-Hereford bus service runs through Glasbury. Brecon to Newtown service stops at Erwood and Boughrood. Builth-to-Hereford service calls at Boughrood village, Erwood and Glasbury Weds and Sats (excluding public holidays)

Easy walking mainly on level field-edge paths and tracks with good views of the Black Mountains. There is a particularly beautiful section on the banks of the Wye between Boughrood and the elegant Llanstephan suspension bridge, and approximately 2.4km on road between Llanstephan Bridge and Erwood Bridge. There are four stiles.

From Glasbury Bridge carefully cross the road and go through the small car park.

Glasbury Scout Hut on the edge of the car park is probably the oldest purpose-built scout hut in Wales still in use. It was opened by the Chief Scout and founder of the scouting movement, Lord Robert Baden-Powell, in the 1920s.

Bear left at the car park entrance and join the road through the village, passing the Maesllwch Arms pub. A short distance beyond the pub the road bears right.

Take the track on the left (SO 175 392) leading into a field, and continue ahead to the track at the far side near the river. Go through the gate and keep on the track, eventually passing **Glasbury Farm**. Once through Glasbury Farm the old lane is lost for the next two fields as the hedge on the left has been removed, but beyond this it reappears. Where the lane bends left (SO 156 384) turn right through a gate that leads to **Pwll-y-baw** ('mucky pool'). Leave the ruins to your right and continue ahead to the B4350 at **Pistyll Farm**.

Turn left and with care follow the road past Glangwye Farm entrance and onto **Boughrood Brest**.

With telephone and post box ahead turn left (SO 147 385) on the track between cottages and continue to open fields. At the end of the second field enter the strip of woodland with the river below. If the river level is not high take the steps down to the water's edge and follow the permissive path along the river and then up to the road (SO 133 387). If the riverside path is flooded go through the gate and follow the Right of Way through **The Old Rectory** garden and grounds to the road.

Turn left and pass through the village of **Boughrood** or, in Welsh, Bochrwyd. Cross the bridge over the Wye, but be careful of traffic as it is narrow.

Bochrwyd (or Bachrwyd) 'Little Ford' Bridge was opened in 1842 to replace a ferry and dangerous ford.

It was paid for by tolls levied on all travellers, the old Toll House still standing on the east side. Tolls were only removed in 1934. The large house on the opposite side of the road is the former Boat Inn and was the only public house in Bochrwyd. The bridge would have been useful in times of flood as the nearest bridges were at Builth upstream or Glasbury downstream.

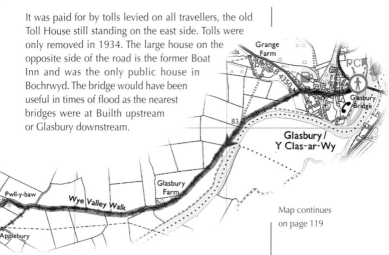

Map continues on page 119

Pass the shop in Boughrood and at the far side of the bridge (SO 129 384) turn right on the tarmaced riverside lane that you follow to the water treatment works where it becomes an unsurfaced footpath.

This is a quite delightful stretch of the **River Wye** offering level walking with no stiles, and the quiet walker can often be rewarded by sightings of heron, kingfisher, common sandpiper, grey wagtail and ducks. Salmon may at times be seen in the river.

The riverside path continues for 2.4km, passing through a series of pedestrian gates and keeping to the field headlands. A small copse is passed within a walled enclosure. This is the family cemetery of the former owners of Llangoed Hall, the large house off to the left amongst trees.
▶ Further along, the path passes the branching track leading to Llangoed Farm, and finally reaches the point where the Sgithwen Brook joins the Wye. The path continues along the brookside, eventually exiting on to the main road (A470) opposite **Trericket Mill** (SO 113 414).

Note the large sweet chestnut trees on the right: some of these are at least 200 years old and were planted by various owners of the estate, along with some oak trees.

117

Llangoed (Michael Mable)

LLANGOED HALL

Now a luxury hotel, it is believed a house or building has occupied this site since AD560. Until 1913 it was known as Llangoed Castle and is thought to have been the site of the first Welsh Parliament, although records are hazy. However, the menhir or standing stone in the field to the south could be megalithic or may mark the site of the meeting, just as Eisteddfods are marked today by standing stones! It is known that a Jacobean-style mansion or house was built around 1633 and went through a series of owners, eventually being bought by the London hatter Archibald Christy in about 1860, and remodelled by Sir Clough Williams-Ellis up till 1914 (his first major architectural commission). The present hall demonstrates much of an Elizabethan style surrounded by walled gardens and magnificent trees, with Williams-Ellis' influence showing through; at one time 20 men were employed to tend the gardens. Williams-Ellis later became the owner and designer of the Italianate village of Portmeirion in North Wales.

Do not be tempted to cross the safety barrier, but walk to the end and turn right. The hill to the left is often the first opportunity for vehicles to pass slow-moving traffic and these often speed down the hill on the offside of the road. Stay on the verge if you intend to continue, but if you intend to visit Trericket Mill (WVW Passport Stamping Station) take extreme care crossing the road.

The route continues northwards to the next junction on the right, signed Llanstephan (SO 112 415). Turn right and cross the elegant Llanstephan suspension bridge. This is a very narrow bridge with no footway and is only wide enough for one vehicle.

Llanstephan Bridge was built in 1922 by David Rowell and Company of Westminster, and is the only wooden-decked vehicular suspension bridge left in Wales. The same company also built the bridge over the Wye at Foy in Herefordshire.

Follow the road uphill to a junction and turn left, following the road until passing below the abutments of a former bridge.

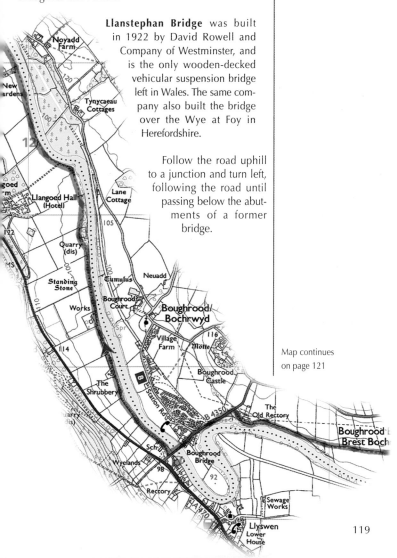

Map continues on page 121

119

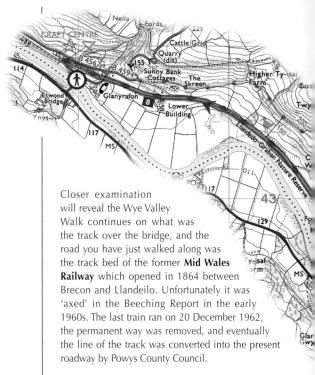

Closer examination will reveal the Wye Valley Walk continues on what was the track over the bridge, and the road you have just walked along was the track bed of the former **Mid Wales Railway** which opened in 1864 between Brecon and Llandeilo. Unfortunately it was 'axed' in the Beeching Report in the early 1960s. The last train ran on 20 December 1962, the permanent way was removed, and eventually the line of the track was converted into the present roadway by Powys County Council.

Continue on this road for 3.5km, crossing a cattle grid and continuing to **Erwood Station Craft Centre and Gallery**.

The roadside verges are a **roadside nature reserve** maintained by Radnorshire Wildlife Trust in cooperation with Powys County Council since 1976. The list of plants and invertebrates is impressive with over 60 species of moths and glow worm recorded.

Just before the car park, the Wye Valley Walk turns left through a wooden pedestrian gate (SO 088 439) and descends to Erwood Bridge on a path with a hedge on the

ERWOOD

Erwood Station Craft Centre and Gallery is open seven days a week from mid February until Christmas Eve, and drinks and homemade cakes can be obtained here. The toilets are available to customers. There are regular exhibitions and craft demonstrations as well as a display recording the history of the station and the railway.

Erwood village is just over half a mile to the left along the A470, but there is no footway and no safe alternative route. Accommodation and refreshments are available in the village, as well as a public telephone box and public toilets.

right, leading into the approach road to Bridge Cottage and then climbing to the roadway. Cross the bridge to meet the main A470 road at the far end.

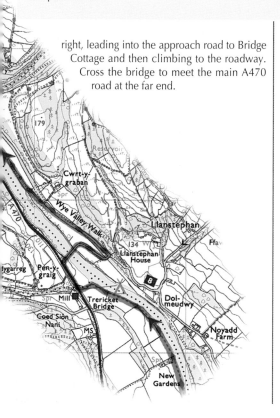

STAGE 13
Erwood to Builth Wells

Start	Erwood Bridge, SO 089 437
Finish	The Groe, Builth Wells, SO 041 511
Distance	11.6km (7¼ miles)
Time	3hr 40min
Height gain	460m (1507ft)
Terrain	Open common land and hillside with some farmland; steep in places; some road walking on quiet lanes
OS map	Explorer 188 Builth Wells
Refreshments	None on route; at Builth Wells
Public toilets	None on route; at Builth Wells
Public transport	Newtown-to-Brecon bus between Erwood and Builth Wells approximately every 2hr (except Suns/public holidays); stops on request. Builth-to-Hereford bus Weds and Sats only (except public holidays) between Builth Wells and Erwood. Railway station on Heart of Wales Line (Shrewsbury to Swansea) at Builth Road about 3.2km from Builth Wells

This stage can best be described as a collection of gradients, mainly 'up'. However, the effort is rewarded with stunning views towards the Black Mountains, Llandeilo and Aberedw Hills and the River Wye below. There are no stiles.

On leaving the A470 at Erwood there is a sharp climb on tarmac to the Twmpath, then a long downhill followed by another sharp climb on tarmac to a more gentle uphill stretch to the common above Bedw, then a reasonably varied but not strenuous walk across the face of Banc y Celyn. From the north end of the common it is mainly downhill but with a sharp uphill from the River Duhonw, then a generally gentle downhill stretch into Builth Wells.

*Above Erwood
(Jon Dixon)*

Erwood Bridge was opened in 1967, replacing an earlier bridge built in the 1860s by the then surveyor of Radnor County Council, Stephen W. Williams. The abutments and piers can still be seen. Williams was a prominent local architect and responsible for the building and restoration of many private and civic buildings in Mid Wales, particularly in Llandrindod Wells and Rhayader.

Crossing the A470, take the minor road opposite (signposted to Gwenddwr) leading to Twmpath Common. The lane soon starts to climb steeply, passing an adjoining footpath on the left and **Ynys-Wye** on the right. Continue onward, crossing a cattle grid onto the common and passing some small rock outcrops, until after 400m there is a wide stony track to the left and public Rights of Way to both left and right (SO 081 436). This elevated position offers superb views of the Wye Valley.

COMMON LAND

This stage of the Walk passes through areas of common land on Twmpath, Little Hill, Banc y Celyn and Allt-mawr, and offers great views over other vast expanses of common land on the east of the Wye Valley. About 8.4

per cent of Wales is registered as common land and because it often has not been improved for agricultural purposes it is of great value for wild-life, including many declining species of farmland birds. A particular habitat known as 'ffridd' – a mixture of bracken and scrub – develops on many upland commons and this is an important habitat for upland birds including whinchat, yellowhammer, linnet, wheatear and redstart.

It is often thought that common land is so called because 'everyone' owns it, but it is 'common land' because historically a number of users may have certain rights over it. Rights of common can include grazing of sheep or cattle (pasturage), taking peat or turf for fuel (turbary), taking wood, gorse or furze (estovers), taking fish (piscary) and grazing pigs on acorns or beech-mast (pannage). Common land is crucially important to many of Wales' farms; without grazing rights many would not be viable.

Take the path on the right, heading northwest and leading down the partially bracken-covered slope across the open common. At the base of the slope a gate and fingerpost mark the point where you leave the common.

LLEWELLYN AP GRUFFYDD

Amongst Aberedw Rocks is a cave known as Llewellyn's Cave, allegedly the hideout of Llewellyn ap Gruffydd, a Welsh prince of Gwynedd, who in the 13th century was at war with the English King Edward I. Being heavily defeated by the English army he allegedly hid in the cave. A local blacksmith turned the shoes of Llewellyn's horse to throw his pursuers off the scent, but the self-same blacksmith betrayed him and on 11 December 1282 Llewellyn and a small band of supporters were ambushed near Irfon Bridge, west of Builth Wells and he was killed. He was decapitated and his head taken to London, but the monks of Cwm Hir Abbey claimed his body and allegedly buried his remains in the abbey, although there is no record or evidence of the burial site today.

Beyond the gate an old trackway can clearly be seen; follow this until it starts to open out. Follow the signed track ahead leading to a gate. Continue on the old lane ahead to a metal footbridge crossing the **Fernant stream**

(SO 072 443) and then follow the track up to a minor road to the right.

Turn left on to the metalled road and follow it to the top of the hill and on to **Little Hill Common**, passing New House on the way. Where the road levels out at the top of the hill fine views of the valley may be gained, including Aberedw Rocks.

Ignore two signed bridleways on the left and continue along the road, following the edge of the common. Keep on this road for almost 1.5km until meeting the junction of the Old Bedw access track (SO 065 462).

Turn left up the track and continue straight ahead on the bridleway leading to the common, ignoring the trackway to Old Bedw on the left. Once on

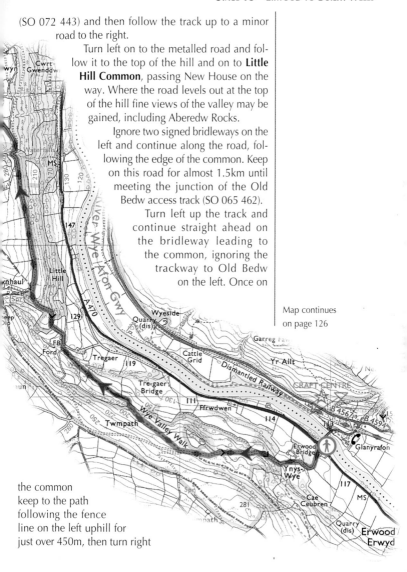

Map continues on page 126

the common keep to the path following the fence line on the left uphill for just over 450m, then turn right

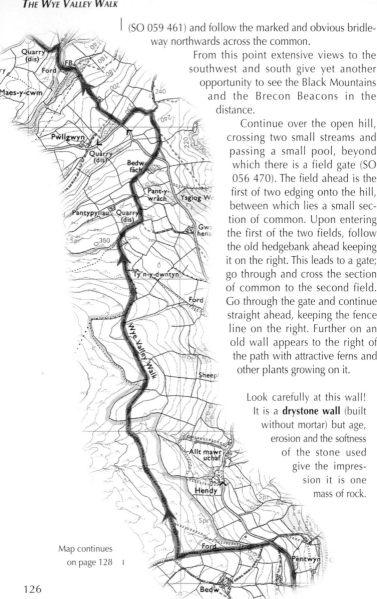

(SO 059 461) and follow the marked and obvious bridleway northwards across the common.

From this point extensive views to the southwest and south give yet another opportunity to see the Black Mountains and the Brecon Beacons in the distance.

Continue over the open hill, crossing two small streams and passing a small pool, beyond which there is a field gate (SO 056 470). The field ahead is the first of two edging onto the hill, between which lies a small section of common. Upon entering the first of the two fields, follow the old hedgebank ahead keeping it on the right. This leads to a gate; go through and cross the section of common to the second field. Go through the gate and continue straight ahead, keeping the fence line on the right. Further on an old wall appears to the right of the path with attractive ferns and other plants growing on it.

Look carefully at this wall! It is a **drystone wall** (built without mortar) but age, erosion and the softness of the stone used give the impression it is one mass of rock.

Map continues
on page 128

Approaching Builth Wells (Michael Mable)

This must be a very old wall and has probably always marked the boundary between the cultivated land and the common.

Continue along the fence line until a gate is reached. Once through the gate turn right and, keeping the fence line on the right, head down the hill until a gate is reached (SO 056 482). Here you finally leave the open hill.

The path now follows a track, in places edged with gorse, and bears left, passing a junction with a footpath on the right. Keep to the track, passing through two gates beyond which is a lane, with good views towards Builth Wells.

At this point the remnants of a small enclosure are marked on the map at **Pant-y-wrâch**, translated as 'witches' hollow', perhaps the site of an abandoned dwelling.

Pass through the gate into the lane and turn right until it meets a minor road at **Bedw-fâch** crossroads (SO 058 488).

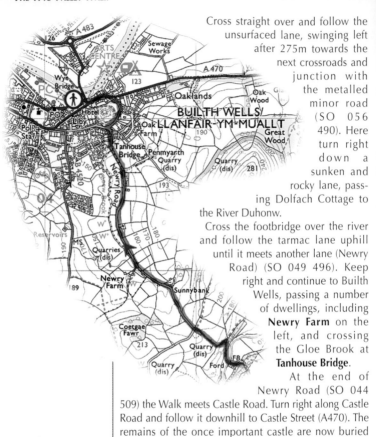

Cross straight over and follow the unsurfaced lane, swinging left after 275m towards the next crossroads and junction with the metalled minor road (SO 056 490). Here turn right down a sunken and rocky lane, passing Dolfach Cottage to the River Duhonw.

Cross the footbridge over the river and follow the tarmac lane uphill until it meets another lane (Newry Road) (SO 049 496). Keep right and continue to Builth Wells, passing a number of dwellings, including **Newry Farm** on the left, and crossing the Gloe Brook at **Tanhouse Bridge**.

At the end of Newry Road (SO 044 509) the Walk meets Castle Road. Turn right along Castle Road and follow it downhill to Castle Street (A470). The remains of the once important castle are now buried under grassy mounds above and to the left.

BUILTH CASTLE

Builth Castle was originally built as a motte-&-bailey castle by Phillip de Braose shortly after the Norman invasion of England in 1066 to control the crossing of the Wye at this spot. In 1277 it was rebuilt as a stone castle by Edward I, although very little trace of this castle remains today.

It was probably used as a convenient stone quarry during the rebuilding of Builth after a devastating fire in 1690 which completely destroyed the town. To reach the Castle Mound there is a marked access path alongside the Lion Hotel.

Turn left along Castle Street to the next road junction, with the Wyeside Arts Centre on the right. Opposite there are two roads – on the left is Broad Street leading to the town centre – but take the road on the right, The Strand, which leads to The Groe, the town park and recreation area. Alternatively continue along Broad Street, where several small roads on the right lead down to The Groe.

BUILTH WELLS

In 1779 the stone bridge over the Wye was built. In the 1820s it was integrated into the construction of the new road linking North and South Wales, thereby making Builth an important junction and centre. In the 1830s a whole new tourist attraction of 'taking the waters' was developed. Park Wells with its saline water and the Glanne Wells with its sulphur springs became popular with Victorians and Edwardians looking for health cures. The coming of the railway in 1860 further aided the town's development, and it was then that 'Wells' was added to its name. It has now gained new importance through the establishment of the permanent showground of the Royal Welsh Agricultural Society, situated at Llanelwedd just across the river. During the annual Royal Welsh Show in July the town can become very busy indeed.

Builth Wells has hotels, B&Bs, shops, banks and ATMs, post office, churches, restaurants and cafés, although most establishments (other than the many public houses and dedicated restaurants) start to close at about 5pm. There are also doctors' surgeries and a small cottage hospital, but the nearest Minor Injuries Unit is at Llandrindod Wells.

STAGE 14
Builth Wells to Newbridge-on-Wye

Start	The Groe, Builth Wells, SO 041 511
Finish	Opposite Pen-y-bont Farm, Newbridge-on-Wye, SO 012 582
Distance	10.8km (6¾ miles)
Time	2hr 45min
Height gain	161m (530ft)
Terrain	Mostly along riverbank; some deviations across farmland and a little woodland
OS map	Explorer 200 Llandrindod Wells & Elan Valley
Refreshments	None on route; Newbridge-on-Wye has two pubs and shop with post office
Public toilets	None on route; at Newbridge-on-Wye
Public transport	Circular bus route via Builth Wells, Llandrindrod Wells, Rhayader and Newbridge-on-Wye and Builth Wells; railway station at Builth Road about 3.2km from Builth Wells
Note	There are no pedestrian bridges across the river between the station at Builth Wells and the Wye Valley Walk on the opposite bank. There is only a road bridge north of Builth (outside the map coverage for this stage).

This stage compensates for the efforts of Stage 13, as it is fairly level with just some gentle upward gradients – generally an easy day's walking, much of it along the river. There are three dog-friendly stiles. At the very end of the section 750m on tarmac on the B4358 should be treated with respect as traffic travels fast along this section.

On entering The Groe, the walk continues along a tree-lined avenue following the edge of the Wye to the con-fluence with the River Irfon ◀, then along the Irfon to a metal suspension bridge (SO 033 514). Cross the bridge to the edge of a minor road, turn right and pass through a

Look out for the 'Leaping Salmon Tree' sculpture on your left!

kissing gate to follow the other side of the Irfon to rejoin the Wye. The path now continues northwards along the river's edge through three fields towards **Penddôl Rocks** (SO 030 522).

The Groe, Builth Wells (Jon Dixon)

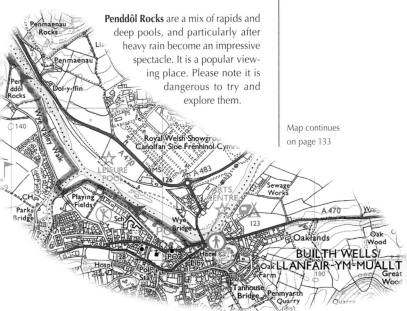

Penddôl Rocks are a mix of rapids and deep pools, and particularly after heavy rain become an impressive spectacle. It is a popular viewing place. Please note it is dangerous to try and explore them.

Map continues on page 133

Leaving the field the path keeps close to the river, passing a small wooden bungalow, then carries on through woods and plantations and under a railway bridge.

The line above is the picturesque **Heart of Wales** Swansea-to-Shrewsbury line and just across the river is Builth Road Station, the nearest railway station to Builth Wells.

Map continues
on page 134

For a short distance beyond the bridge the path runs parallel with a lane serving Dolyrerw Farm and Rhosferig Lodge.

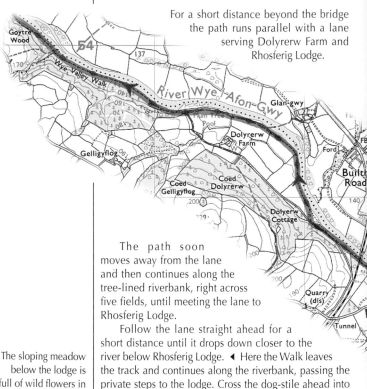

The path soon moves away from the lane and then continues along the tree-lined riverbank, right across five fields, until meeting the lane to Rhosferig Lodge.

Follow the lane straight ahead for a short distance until it drops down closer to the river below Rhosferig Lodge. ◄ Here the Walk leaves the track and continues along the riverbank, passing the private steps to the lodge. Cross the dog-stile ahead into the first of two fields backed by conifers. In the second field, where in places small areas of hardwoods have

The sloping meadow below the lodge is full of wild flowers in the summer.

132

been planted, the path runs alongside the river. At the end of the second field there is a footbridge with stile crossing a small stream beyond which lies **Goytre Wood**.

On entering the wood (SO 003 539) keep right on the lower of the two paths available, and follow the riverbank. Within the wood the path stays close to the river, but does climb above it for part of the way; however it drops back down to the river as the path leaves the wood. Keeping to the riverside, cross four fields beyond which the path enters the first of two adjoining conifer plantations, the second of which is quite narrow, with the path generally moving away from and above the river.

The path now enters a broadleaved wood, keeping to the top edge. A cedar-shingled bungalow is situated at the edge of the wood on the riverside. Start to descend in the direction of the lodge but soon bear away to a gate in the northeast corner of the wood. Leave the woodland, cross the stream (SO 003 554) and carry straight on up a slight incline until the field levels out. Now bear left to follow the fence line alongside the woodland until the next gate is reached.

Once in the next field, follow the fence on the right and head for the gate across the field, just to the left of the buildings of **Porthllwyd Farm**.

The large house on the left is **Bryn-wern Hall**, built in 1886 to the design of local architect Stephen W. Williams, the builder of Erwood Bridge (Stage 13) and whose work we will encounter again later on the Walk.

Pass through the gate and continue with the barn on the right; turn right into the yard for a few metres and take the first gate on the left. Cross a small field leading to a small woodland, beyond which lies a minor road.

Map continues
on page 135

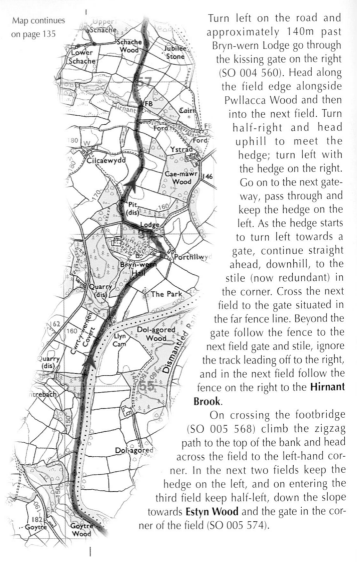

Turn left on the road and approximately 140m past Bryn-wern Lodge go through the kissing gate on the right (SO 004 560). Head along the field edge alongside Pwllacca Wood and then into the next field. Turn half-right and head uphill to meet the hedge; turn left with the hedge on the right. Go on to the next gateway, pass through and keep the hedge on the left. As the hedge starts to turn left towards a gate, continue straight ahead, downhill, to the stile (now redundant) in the corner. Cross the next field to the gate situated in the far fence line. Beyond the gate follow the fence to the next field gate and stile, ignore the track leading off to the right, and in the next field follow the fence on the right to the **Hirnant Brook**.

On crossing the footbridge (SO 005 568) climb the zigzag path to the top of the bank and head across the field to the left-hand corner. In the next two fields keep the hedge on the left, and on entering the third field keep half-left, down the slope towards **Estyn Wood** and the gate in the corner of the field (SO 005 574).

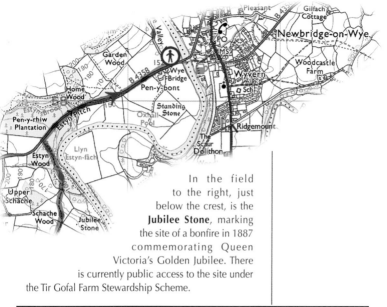

In the field to the right, just below the crest, is the **Jubilee Stone**, marking the site of a bonfire in 1887 commemorating Queen Victoria's Golden Jubilee. There is currently public access to the site under the Tir Gofal Farm Stewardship Scheme.

NEWBRIDGE-ON-WYE

Newbridge-on-Wye lies over the Wye Bridge. On the right of the bridge is the original ford that was used by drovers to drive their cattle over the river to the markets in the Midlands and London.

There are two public houses and a shop with post office in Newbridge-on-Wye, and accommodation providers.

Enter the wood. After a few yards there is a fork in the path. Keep left and carry on, over a series of boardwalks. Soon, at another fork, take the path to the left that leads to the B4358 (SO 004 577). Turn right and follow the road towards Newbridge-on-Wye, about 750m.

STAGE 15
Newbridge-on-Wye to Rhayader

Start	Opposite Pen-y-bont Farm, Newbridge-on-Wye, SO 012 582
Finish	Rhayader crossroads, SN 970 680
Distance	15.5km (9½ miles)
Time	4hr 45min
Height gain	511m (1677ft)
Terrain	Mainly farmland and woodland, some quite steep; highest point 378m (1240ft)
OS map	Explorer 200 Llandrindod Wells & Elan Valley
Refreshments	None on route; petrol station with shop, post office and café on A470 near Llanwrthwl about 1km from route; Rhayader has shops, pubs and cafés
Public toilets	None on route; at petrol station near Llanwrthwl and in Rhayader
Public transport	Rhayader, Llanwrthwl (at end of bridge on A470) and Newbridge-on-Wye (New Inn) on Rhayader-to-Builth Wells bus route

This stage is a pleasant mix of farmland, old roads, woodland and open hill, with a steep climb towards the end over Graig Allt-y-bont, then an exciting suspension bridge over the Afon Elan before reaching Rhayader. Part of the stage is shared with National Cycle Route 8. There are no stiles.

Just before reaching the Wye Bridge turn left, opposite **Pen-y-bont Farm**, along a minor road signposted **Llysdinam**. Go past the entrance to Llysdinam House, turn right (SO 007 588) immediately before Dol Cottage and follow the footpath north.

The route now follows the left-hand edge of two fields before it reaches **Estyn-gwyn Brook**. Cross the footbridge, and then after a short distance through a narrow strip of woodland cross a second footbridge and go into a field. Head for the gate across this field and pass through a series of gates keeping close to the fence line on the right until the track to **Ty'n y-coed** is reached. Turn left along the track to the end of Ty'n y-coed Wood, then turn right (SO 006 594) along the end of the wood and into the next field. Follow the hedge on the left to the far corner of the field, via sections of boardwalk. From the corner of this field pass through a gate and cross a ditch into the next field. Turn right and carry on to meet the field boundary. Follow this boundary until it turns right. Then head for the gate across the field, and looking towards a dingle ahead. Continue diagonally to the left to the fingerpost on the edge of the dingle. The path leads down the dingle and across a footbridge.

Map continues on page 139

Map continues on page 140

Head back up the slope and enter the corner of the adjoining field via a gate. Keep close to the hedge line on the right, heading north, via a boardwalk to the minor road (SO 003 601).

Go straight on and keep on the road until it turns left (SO 008 603) over a small stone bridge, passing the turn for Tycwtta Farm. The track now becomes unsurfaced and leads to **Ty'n-y-lôn Wood**. Keep to the lower edge of the wood until the track emerges onto the open common.

Abergwesyn Common (Michael Mable)

The hill to the left is **Trembyd**; at 475m high it marks the eastern edge of one of the largest areas of open upland and common land in Wales, stretching westwards towards Abergwesyn and the valley of the Afon Tywi. Much of the land is owned by the National Trust.

The route follows the track for 2km. Keep to the track, passing two small plantations between which fine views can be gained across the valley including Doldowlod House.

Doldowlod House

can be clearly seen in the valley and was designed by Stephen W Williams. James Watt, the inventor of an efficient steam engine, bought the estate after he retired and much improved it. The house was then owned by James Watt Jnr, also an engineer, who designed and built the south part of the hall.

At the end of the second plantation leave the open hill through a gate and turn left onto a metalled lane (SN 988 623).

Map continues on page 144

The route now keeps to the lane all the way to **Llanwrthwl** village, a distance of 2.4km. Passing **Hodrid House** the lane crosses a small section of common. Once past the common the lane moves closer to the river, which can be seen to the right at the base of the wooded slope. Shortly after passing a house on the left, called Craig-Llyn, the lane starts to move back a little way from the river, passing an old mill, bridge and chapel and then carries on to **Llanwrthwl**.

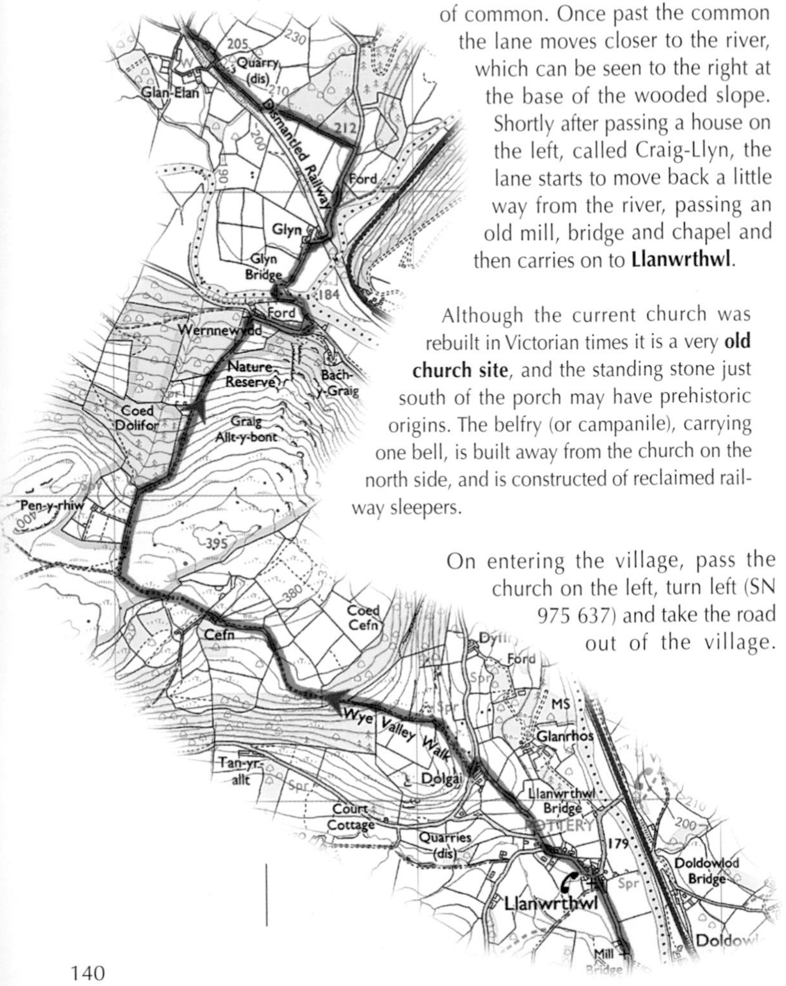

Although the current church was rebuilt in Victorian times it is a very **old church site**, and the standing stone just south of the porch may have prehistoric origins. The belfry (or campanile), carrying one bell, is built away from the church on the north side, and is constructed of reclaimed railway sleepers.

On entering the village, pass the church on the left, turn left (SN 975 637) and take the road out of the village.

Immediately past the last building on the right (the old school), turn right and leave the road at the first bend and keep straight ahead up an old track (SN 973 638) to meet a minor road at **Dolgai Farm**.

Turn left along the road for just over 45m and turn right up the farm track (SN 971 640). As height is gained so the views of the valley and its surrounding hills become more impressive.

Progressing up the track, it turns left with the Right of Way cutting the corner across the field and keeping alongside the old wall leading to a gate. Beyond the gate lies Cefn Wood. Continue along the track through the wood and across a field to a gateway. The track now becomes more enclosed, passing a small quarry on the right just before reaching **Cefn Farm**.

Pass through the farmyard (making sure to shut the gates) to the field beyond. Once in the field the track splits. Follow the track straight ahead and through the gate (SN 961 646). The track now continues across open hill, named **Graig Allt-y-bont**.

This is the eastern outlier of the **Carngafallt Nature Reserve**, owned and managed by the Royal Society for the Protection of Birds. The reserve covers 368ha and hosts a variety of birds. On Graig Allt-y-bont the species most likely to be seen are red kite, buzzard, stonechat, whinchat and redstart in summer. During the colder months, you may also come across – in addition to the first three species above – woodcock and migrant thrushes such as fieldfare and redwing.

In a short distance the track forks again. Turn right here, passing **Pen-y-rhiw** on the left and keeping to the edge of the common, to follow the path down the slope. ▶

Dolifor Wood, on the left, is owned by the Woodland Trust and a short detour can be taken through it to rejoin the Wye Valley Walk on the minor road at the bottom of the hill. The wood contains an unusual mixture of trees – native birch, alder and oak –together with

Enjoy extensive views north, across the valley to the old quarry and Gwastedyn Hill, and to Rhayader, with the confluence of the River Elan and River Wye in the foreground.

Glyn Bridge (Michael Mable)

more exotic species planted by the former owner with the intention of creating an arboretum. The wood had previously been open woodland grazing dominated by oak, birch and alder and was very boggy.

At the lower edge of the common a narrow lane leads to a minor road. At **Wernnewydd House** (SN 964 655) turn right along the road for just over 180m and take the track on the left. This track leads to the narrow and swaying suspension bridge across the Afon Elan, **Glyn Bridge** (SN 965 656), at the old fording point just before it joins the River Wye.

This is one of several **similar suspension** bridges existing in this part of the Wye Valley that were built in the 1960s by a local Newbridge-on-Wye company.

Once across the bridge turn right and join the lane to **Glyn Farm**. On approaching the farm pass through the gate and bear right, continuing on the lane, between the abutments of an old railway bridge, where it becomes metalled. Keep to the lane for just under 370m and then turn left along an unsurfaced lane (SN 968 661). This lane eventually meets and runs parallel to the old railway line. At the next junction keep right (SN 963 664) (turning left here passes under the railway line to Glan-Elan Farm). The route now passes between farm buildings to another junction; keep right again here. ▶

Please note the course of the old railway is not a Right of Way.

After turning right, follow the lane for 800m to its junction with a metalled minor road (SN 966 671) and continue straight on. This minor road leads to Rhayader, passing the properties of **New House Farm** on the right and Glanserth on the left. Here you have a choice. Either continue on the road to **Cwmdeuddwr** and take a short street up to the right of the Triangle Public House that dates from the 16th century and was an old drovers' stopping place. Turn right at the main road and follow it into **Rhayader**, crossing the bridge over the River Wye. Or take an attractive alternative path by following the fingerpost on the left in front of Glanserth (SN 967 675) down

*Approaching Rhayader
(Michael Mable)*

through Cwmdeuddwr churchyard, passing the old parish pound where stray animals would have been held until released to their owner on payment of a fine. Bear right at the main road and follow it into Rhayader, as on the main route above.

When the Wye reaches Rhayader it encounters a rocky channel and the resulting waterfalls gave the town its Welsh name of **Rhaeadr Gwy** meaning 'the waterfall of the Wye'. The falls below the bridge are impressive, especially when the river is in spate.

RHAYADER

Rhayader today is a friendly, busy little town at a crossroads between Aberystwyth, the English Midlands and South Wales. However, between 1839 and 1844 South and Mid Wales witnessed a unique phenomenon of social unrest, triggered by the construction of turnpike roads on which tolls were levied on travellers and their animals. In some places passing through an area or returning along the same route could involve paying tolls twice or sometimes more. In a series of attacks on tollgates and bars – known as the 'Rebecca Riots' – the attackers dressed as women to hide their identity. The leader, who invariably rode a horse, was referred to as Rebecca, and 'her' followers as her 'daughters'.

Although the majority of attacks occurred in Carmarthenshire, Pembrokeshire and Cardiganshire, in the autumn of 1843 Rhayader became the focus of attention. No less than six toll gates had been erected around Rhayader and on Friday, 22 September a 'Rebecca' attack was made on the first gate on North Road. The attacks went on throughout the autumn and winter, with the result that the Militia was called out, and even members of the London Metropolitan Police were employed to restore order. The last attack in the Rhayader area came in September 1844. A Commission of Enquiry was set up to investigate the causes of the unrest and eventually the tolls were lifted when the roads were taken over by the new Highway Authorities.

Rhayader has a wealth of hotels and other accommodation opportunities, with restaurants, cafés, several banks with ATMs, shops and a post office. There is a leisure centre with swimming pool and a livestock market is held on Fridays. The main roads through the town are North, South, East and West Streets!

Rhayader (Michael Mable)

STAGE 16

Rhayader to Llangurig

Start	Rhayader crossroads, SN 970 680
Finish	Llangurig Bridge, Llangurig, SN 907 796
Distance	19.4km (12 miles)
Time	6hr 10min
Height gain	665m (2182ft)
Terrain	Woodland, open hillside; three sections of minor road
OS maps	Explorers 200 Llandrindod Wells & Elan Valley, 214 Llanidloes & Newtown
Refreshments	Gilfach Nature Reserve Discovery Centre (light refreshments when open); Llangurig has two pubs and shop with post office
Public toilets	In car park by Rhayader Leisure Centre; at Gilfach Farm Nature Reserve Discovery Centre (when open)
Public transport	Twice daily bus service Rhayader to Llangurig Mon–Sat

A beautiful stage of the Walk venturing into the uplands of Mid Wales with views towards Plynlimon. It includes sections of high-level walking over open countryside, up to 480m, and some woodland walking. It passes through Gilfach Nature Reserve so allow time to enjoy this special place. There are several stiles to be negotiated between the Dernol Valley and Llangurig. If a lower-level alternative is preferred the quiet, attractive road on the west of the River Wye can be followed between Rhayader and Llangurig.

From the clock tower in Rhayader walk along North Street as far as the Leisure Centre (WVW Passport Stamping Station). Turn right on the B4518 signposted to St Harmon. Stay on the right-hand side of the road for about 460m before turning left up a minor road (SN 972 685), passing the school and pottery workshop.

Carry on uphill and downhill as the road winds through an oak wood and climbs past **Middle Nantserth Farm**. After another 800m, at the crest, a bridleway leaves the road on the right and a footpath on the left. Continue past these, following the road downhill, and take the next turn on the left (SN 971 708) just before **Tynshimley**, leading onto an enclosed track.

Pass through three fields, keeping to the right-hand edge. To the left above the track in the third field are the remains of a **house platform**.

Map continues on page 149

147

MEDIEVAL FARMSTEADS

'House platforms' are found all over the uplands of Wales. They are the sites of medieval farmsteads, constructed by digging into the hillside and pushing the resulting soil downhill to create a terrace. Better quality buildings had a gutter on the upside to drain water away, but many were simply built with their roofs resting on the upward slope. It was the origin of the Welsh long-house, where humans lived on the uphill side of the building and animals on the lower side so that manure drained away downhill. Many modern farmsteads can be identified as being built on house platforms of medieval origin. These sites were not only used by peasant farmers; many of the minor gentry also occupied similar buildings as recorded by Gerald of Wales (Giraldus Cambrensis) during his travels through Wales in the 12th century.

From here there is an excellent view of the Marteg Valley and surrounding hills.

Go straight on along a rough hillside with gorse bushes, still keeping the fence line on the right. Pass through a gate leading onto the open hillside. ◄

Carry straight on for a few metres and then bear left and shortly turn right, following a path heading diagonally down the hillside to **Gilfach Nature Reserve**, owned and managed by the Radnorshire Wildlife Trust. Ignore the paths leading off to the left, and head downhill towards the farm buildings glimpsed in front of a small stand of conifers.

Lower down, the track becomes more obvious and after passing through a gate, a made-up path leads to the farmyard of **Gilfach Farm** (SN 965 717) which houses a unique medieval Welsh longhouse, restored using some of the surviving original features. In the barn opposite there is a Discovery Centre with a good amount of information about the reserve. Picnic benches, light refreshments and toilets (seasonal) are also available. A WVW Passport Stamping Station is located in the byre at the side of the farmhouse. This is where the animals used to live and now provides wet weather cover all year round for visitors.

The Wye Valley Walk leaves the farmyard to the left on a metalled lane leading down to the Afon Marteg. Cross over the bridge (SN 962 717) past the otter hide

and turn immediately left following the Nature Trail (way-marked with yellow pawprints) along the riverbank.

The Longhouse, Gilfach (Michael Mable)

This **river section**, part pastoral and part rocky and dramatic, allows particularly good sightings of dippers and grey wagtails. In summer look out for increasingly scarce fritillary butterflies; the bloody-nosed beetle, a slow-moving pure black beetle often found on grassy tracks that if alarmed exudes a red fluid from its joints and mouth, hence its name; and glow worms on the railway track after sunset. The female activates a chemical in her abdomen which glows in the dark to attract a mate.

Note: your OS map may show the old route

Map continues on page 151

Gilfach Farm Nature Reserve (Jon Dixon)

GILFACH NATURE RESERVE

Gilfach is overlooked by a Bronze Age burial mound, deserted house sites, green lanes and ancient stone walls, set within a landscape comprising high moorland, enclosed meadows, oak woodlands and the rocky, tumbling waters of the Afon Marteg. The Gilfach Nature Reserve covers over 162ha and is a Site of Special Scientific Interest (SSSI). It is a good place to see many species of birds, and mammals such as otter, polecat and stoat. The Marteg Tunnel provides an important habitat for bats. Bats are legally protected and are not to be disturbed. Salmon can sometimes be seen in autumn struggling up the Afon Marteg attempting to reach their spawning grounds. A variety of trails explore the nature reserve, including part of the Monks Trod that was the main route between the Cistercian abbeys of Cwm Hir and Strata Florida.

Look left at the kissing gate to see the impressive railway bridge arch over the river.

After about 800m the trail leaves the river and snakes up to a railway embankment (SN 959 714) To the right is the sealed western entrance of the 305m-long Marteg Tunnel, part of the old Mid Wales Railway that existed for 99 years and closed in 1962. Go straight across the old railway line and descend on a path to a kissing gate. ◄

Follow a grassy path uphill towards the road then, bearing left on to the path running along the hill between the river and the road, continue until you reach the road near the car park. From here follow the road past the car park, passing through the gate at the side of the cattle grid to reach the main road at **Pont Marteg**.

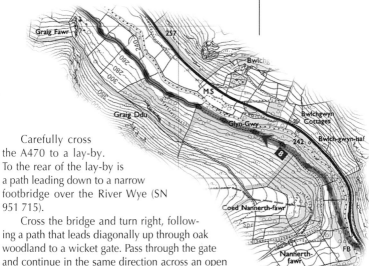

Carefully cross the A470 to a lay-by. To the rear of the lay-by is a path leading down to a narrow footbridge over the River Wye (SN 951 715).

Cross the bridge and turn right, following a path that leads diagonally up through oak woodland to a wicket gate. Pass through the gate and continue in the same direction across an open field leading up to a track. Turn right along the track and continue through further fields until a narrow metalled road is joined (SN 948 721).

Map continues
on page 153

*Pont Marteg
(Michael Mable)*

151

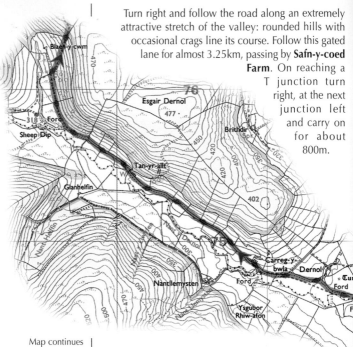

Turn right and follow the road along an extremely attractive stretch of the valley: rounded hills with occasional crags line its course. Follow this gated lane for almost 3.25km, passing by **Safn-y-coed Farm**. On reaching a T junction turn right, at the next junction left and carry on for about 800m.

Map continues on page 155

Parts of the route to Llangurig now cross high open countryside. **If a lower-level alternative is preferred stay on the road for 6km (3.75 miles) to Llangurig (marked in blue leaving the route on this map and returning on the next one).**

As the road to Llangurig turns right, go straight on heading up the Dernol Valley (SN 918 745) This is a gated road, so please leave all gates as you find them. Cross two cattle grids and pass the farm **Carreg-y-bwla**. The gated road continues up by **Tan-yr-allt**. A gate at this point is succeeded by another gate after about 365m later. Some 180m beyond this bear right off the road (SN 896 757) onto a grass track running beneath a birch wood that is full of bluebells in springtime.

Welsh stone wall near Safn-y-coed (Michael Mable)

Approaching the second old hedge line rising from the valley, branch right (SN 895 761) and climb steeply towards a gate leading to an enclosed track going up the mountainside. Climb up through two more gates, after which the gradient eases into an open field. ▶

Turn half-left and cross the field diagonally, passing through an area of marshy land and heading for a stile just to the right of some sheep pens (SN 896 767). To the right Bryn Titli Wind Farm can be

Looking back there is a good view of the valley, dominated by the conifers of Coed-y-Trafelgwyn seemingly spilling into Nant Blaen-y-cwm.

153

*Dernol Valley
(Michael Mable)*

seen. Cross the stile and head along the ridgetop, towards a gate and a stile.

Bryn Titli Wind Farm was completed in 1994 and was one of the first to be constructed in Wales. It covers an area of 1000ha and has 22 turbines. Grazing has been reduced and the land is managed for conservation and monitored by the Countryside Council for Wales (CCW) and the RSPB. The output is alleged to be 9.9 million megawatts (or enough to power 5300 homes). By modern standards these turbines are now regarded as 'small'.

This gate leads onto open land with a small unnamed summit ahead.

On the map some of the features on this hillside are distinguished by the Welsh word esgair, meaning 'ridge' or 'spine'.

At 478m this is one of the **highest points** on the walk and stunning views are on offer on a clear day. Plynlimon, source of the river Wye, can now be seen in the distance towards the northwest. ◀

Aim for a point on the right-hand shoulder of the hill, ignoring a track that skirts the left-hand edge. When adjacent to the summit turn half-right and go downhill to a gate at a corner of a field. Go through the next field and

Coed-y-Trafel

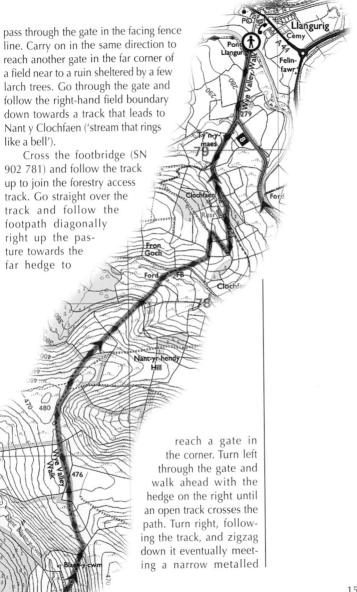

pass through the gate in the facing fence line. Carry on in the same direction to reach another gate in the far corner of a field near to a ruin sheltered by a few larch trees. Go through the gate and follow the right-hand field boundary down towards a track that leads to Nant y Clochfaen ('stream that rings like a bell').

Cross the footbridge (SN 902 781) and follow the track up to join the forestry access track. Go straight over the track and follow the footpath diagonally right up the pasture towards the far hedge to

reach a gate in the corner. Turn left through the gate and walk ahead with the hedge on the right until an open track crosses the path. Turn right, following the track, and zigzag down it eventually meeting a narrow metalled

155

THE CLOCHFAEN

The Clochfaen is an impressive building. Originally a farm, it became the home of a priest-turned-squire, and has been a school, a hotel and a grand holiday home. The house was based on an original longhouse pattern and grew in importance to be known as Clochfaen Hall or Court. It has changed hands several times and was destroyed by fire in 1760 in a possible arson attack. Today's building reflects two major periods: the older part was rebuilt after the fire, but the newer section on the left was started in 1913–14 to the plans of Arts and Crafts Movement architect William Arthur Smith Benson. Unfortunately, a major part of the workforce went off to fight in World War I; construction only continued because of the Verney family's royal connections giving them access to scarce materials. The workforce consisted of craftsmen too old for the Forces assisted by 16-year-old boys recruited from Shrewsbury. After the extension was completed, Clochfaen was visited in 1917 by the young Prince Albert (later King George VI, father of the present Queen Elizabeth) who was sent here after the Battle of Jutland to recuperate from the effects of a duodenal ulcer. The estate was sold in 1927 to the Stirk family of Birmingham who used the house as a holiday home, rented it out as a school and a hotel, and latterly as home for several members of the family. After years of neglect the present owner has rebuilt the interior, re-roofed the extensions and generally preserved the building for the future. The Clochfaen stands in 8ha of garden and woodland.

road (SN 906 785). Bear right down this road, passing the buildings of **Clochfaen**.

*Buildings of Clochfaen
(Michael Mable)*

LLANGURIG

It is well worth venturing into the village of Llangurig – the first village on the River Wye as it flows south from the slopes of Plynlimon. The parish church, dedicated to St Curig, a Celtic saint, was founded before AD550 and had connections with the monasteries at Cwm Hir and Strata Florida. Norman invaders (who did not recognise Celtic saints) changed the dedication to St Cyricus the Martyr, thereby confusing the two saints in local folklore. The church was partially rebuilt and remodelled by that great Victorian church rebuilder (some may say 'destroyer') Sir Gilbert Scott RA. The church has some fine woodwork (including a rood screen) and stained glass windows, due in large part to the Chevalier Jacob Youde William Lloyd, an ordained Anglican priest who became a Roman Catholic priest and a Knight of Saint Gregory. He left the Church on inheriting Clochfaen and set about improving the estate. How well he did can be judged by the work in the church and the red granite memorial on Llangurig's main street. Look for the Verney-Lloyd cipher on buildings in Llangurig.

Llangurig has a village shop and post office, two public houses offering refreshments and accommodation, and other B&B opportunities.

Carry on along this metalled road until it joins the road leading left into Llangurig. The Wye Valley Walk leaves the road just before the bridge over the river (SN 908 796).

*Llangurig Church
(Michael Mable)*

STAGE 17

Llangurig to Rhyd-y-benwch
(Hafren Forest car park)

Start	Llangurig Bridge, Llangurig, SN 907 796
Finish	Rhyd-y-benwch (Hafren Forest car park), Llanidloes, SN 857 869
Distance	19.6km (12¼ miles)
Time	5hr 45min
Height gain	468m (1534ft)
Terrain	Farmland, open hill and woodland to Pont Rhydgaled; stone track to 479m before descent through Hafren Forest to Rhyd-y-benwch
OS map	Explorer 214 Llanidloes & Newtown
Refreshments	None on route
Public toilets	At Rhyd-y-benwch (seasonal)
Public transport	National Express bus Aberystwyth to Birmingham and London passes through Llangurig (Black Lion/post office) and Llanidloes (Gro car park); only specified stops, book in advance. Daily Aberystwyth-to-Llanidloes bus (except Suns/public holidays) stops in Llangurig. Bus between Llangurig and Rhayader twice daily Mon–Sat

The last stage of the Walk is a full day, but consolation lies in the extensive views across the Welsh hills and the quiet woodland and farmland. It is possible to split the day as there is a car parking area at Pont Rhydgaled, but this is not public and permission should be sought from the farm opposite. The rest of the Walk is over rising open country and forest with extensive views and interesting industrial archaeology. Motor rallying events take place at Sweet Lamb and in Hafren Forest and could affect your enjoyment: contacts for more information are given later in this section.

Please note there is no public transport from the end of the Walk at Rhyd-y-benwch to Llanidloes, although local taxi services will collect walkers from Hafren Forest car park at Rhyd-y-benwch. There is also no mobile phone reception at the finish so make arrangements beforehand. There are several stiles on the first part of this stage up to Pont Rhydgaled; the rest is stile-free.

To continue the Walk without visiting Llangurig, turn left before the bridge onto a surfaced road leading uphill to **Llwyn-gwyn Farm**. The road eventually bears right and approaches the farmyard. Glance down right for good views of the River Wye. Turn left (SN 901 794) just before entering the farmyard and skirt around the farm buildings onto a stony farm track. Still climbing, go past two communication towers to a pair of gates at the top of the track (SN 899 793). Pass through the left-hand gate leading onto open countryside.

Continue with the gradient, which soon eases; down to the left is a small stream, Nant-y-Maes. Stay on the ridge, ignoring the track going down to the ruins of **Warren House** on the left. At the end of this ridge turn right downhill, well before the small wood ahead, to meet a gate in the corner of the fence (SN 891 791). Follow the track through two gates and then go down a steep incline to the bottom of the field keeping the fence on the right, and turn left alongside a small plantation.

Map continues
on page 160

159

Carry on with the fence line on the right until a stile is reached. Cross this and follow the fence line down to an old sunken lane. Turn left along the lane, crossing a stile, and after a few yards bear diagonally right across a small field to reach a stile and small bridge. Turn right in the next field and follow the right-hand field boundary down to reach a wide stony forestry access track (SN 886 796).

Turn right and continue along the road passing **Pen-y-rhos**. Turn left at the road junction and follow the road as it loops past **Troed-yr-esgair**. As the road swings to the left, carry straight on over a cattle grid to a farm track leading down to **Pen-y-geulan Farm** (SN 887 799).

Keeping to the left and above the farm buildings of Pen-y-geulan, follow the track through a gate and over a cattle grid. Continue along the track until a path on the right is marked (SN 881 800). This loops down towards the river. The Walk now passes through several riverside fields before reaching **Ty-mawr Farm**. Follow a track around the edge of Ty-mawr, passing a large bridge on the right. The track bears left, leaving the River Wye, and follows the **Nant Ty-mawr**. Take the right-hand fork (SN 871 807) and cross the

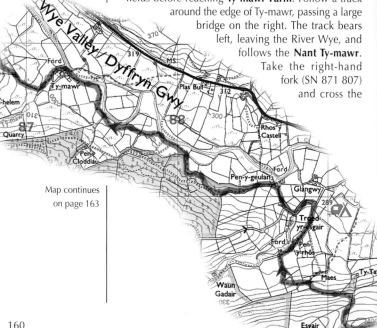

Map continues
on page 163

stream, following the path uphill to a gate. Turn right and follow the track leading downhill, passing an old barn.

Nanty Farm (Michael Mable)

At the bottom of this track turn left, and almost immediately bear right towards the riverbank and a stile (SN 865 813). The path loops around in front of **Hendre**, before crossing the drive and turning right at the fence. Continue uphill to cross a footbridge and stile leading into a field. Proceed through four fields before reaching a gate. There is a choice of routes at this point: a riverside or woodland option (SN 859 814).

To follow the riverside path bear right down the hillside towards a gate. Turn left and follow the path that soon leads onto a farm track running near the river. When the track bends sharp left take the stile on the right and follow the riverbank to the next stile that leads back into a field with a bridge crossing the **Nant-y-Cwm**. Continue through further fields to reach a large footbridge over the River Wye. Don't cross this, but follow the top of the flood bank around to reach the forest road.

To follow the higher woodland path bear half-left once through the gate and head uphill towards the hedge line. Pass through the hedge line and continue diagonally uphill to reach a gate providing access into the woodland.

Map continues on
page 164

Turn right and follow the forestry track. At a T-junction turn right and cross the **Nant-y-Cwm**. At the next fork of tracks keep left and follow the main forestry track. Ignore the next right-hand turn down to Nanty. Continue along the track until a turn on the right leads downhill back towards the river and rejoins the riverside route (SN 851 821).

The Wye Valley Walk now continues along this track close to the river.

Turn right at the next crossroads (SN 840 824) and cross the Afon Tarrenig on a footbridge, just before it joins the River Wye.

At the A44 at **Pont Rhydgaled** (SN 840 827) cross the road carefully. Turn left and immediately take the entrance road on the right leading into a farmyard. Go through the farmyard and climb gently uphill along the broad, stone-surfaced track, with the River Wye down below.

As well as a big sheep farm, this is also home of the **Sweet Lamb Rally Complex** and some major events take place here. To find out more visit **www.sweetlamb. co.uk** or tel: 01686 440208.

LOCAL INDUSTRIES

Mining for silver and lead was a major industry in this area through the 18th and 19th centuries, although there is evidence that lead was mined in the Middle Ages and even earlier. In this valley there were no less than four mines working mainly for lead, although the Nant-yr-Eira Mine also produced copper. All the mines closed in the late 19th century except Nant Iago, which finally closed in 1917. There are many old mine shafts in the valley so please keep to the track.

Several flumes and rain gauges are also passed. The Centre of Ecology and Hydrology is undertaking a national research project comparing the Wye and Severn headwaters. Please do not approach or touch the equipment.

After 1.25km cross the river and continue on the main track, passing two roads coming in from the right. Continue on the track towards some stock sheds, ignoring several incoming roads. Pass through gates and continue up the track until a large parking area is reached at the Sweet Lamb Rally Complex (SN 827 850).

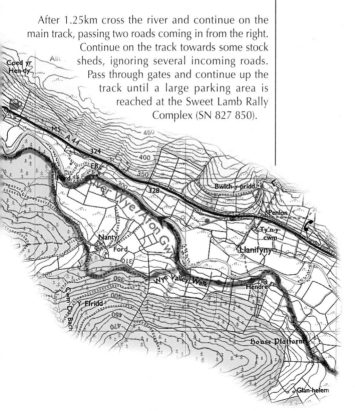

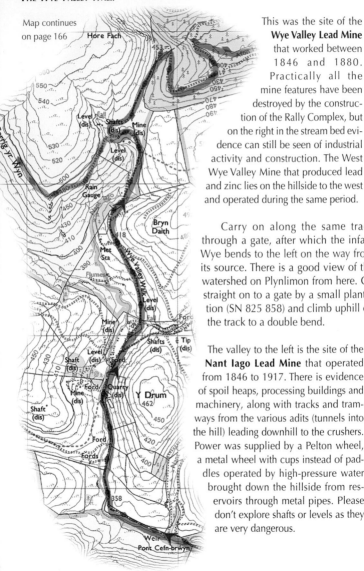

Map continues
on page 166

This was the site of the **Wye Valley Lead Mine** that worked between 1846 and 1880. Practically all the mine features have been destroyed by the construction of the Rally Complex, but on the right in the stream bed evidence can still be seen of industrial activity and construction. The West Wye Valley Mine that produced lead and zinc lies on the hillside to the west and operated during the same period.

Carry on along the same track through a gate, after which the infant Wye bends to the left on the way from its source. There is a good view of the watershed on Plynlimon from here. Go straight on to a gate by a small plantation (SN 825 858) and climb uphill on the track to a double bend.

The valley to the left is the site of the **Nant Iago Lead Mine** that operated from 1846 to 1917. There is evidence of spoil heaps, processing buildings and machinery, along with tracks and tramways from the various adits (tunnels into the hill) leading downhill to the crushers. Power was supplied by a Pelton wheel, a metal wheel with cups instead of paddles operated by high-pressure water brought down the hillside from reservoirs through metal pipes. Please don't explore shafts or levels as they are very dangerous.

Follow the road, bending left and then right.

A track to the left (SN 825 863) on the second bend leads to a **superb viewpoint** looking towards the source of the Wye (another 2km NW at SN 802 872): well worth the detour. According to legend, the Rivers Wye, Severn and Rheidol once discussed the best route from Plynlimon to the sea. The Wye chose the prettiest route!

The uppermost reaches of the River Wye (Michael Mable)

PLYNLIMON AND THE SOURCE OF THE WYE

Plynlimon is one of the most important upland areas for nature conservation in Wales, particularly for its heathland and birdlife. The main vegetation types are acid grassland, blanket bog and dwarf-shrub heath. Birds of prey seen here include buzzard, kestrel, red kite and peregrine falcon.

The land over to the source of the Wye is now designated as Open Access land under the Countryside and Rights of Way Act 2000 for England and Wales and is open for the public to walk over. However, it is boggy, uneven and not way-marked, and should only be attempted by well-equipped and experienced walkers.

Looking towards the source (Powys County Council)

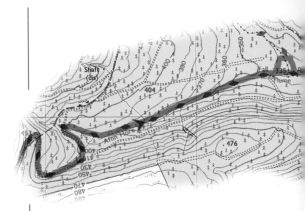

The Wye Valley Walk continues climbing on the main track, soon reaching a high point (479m) from which the extent of **Hafren Forest** can be appreciated.

HAFREN FOREST

The forest takes its name from Afon Hafren (River Severn) that rises in a deep, blanket-peat bog, 1.25km outside its boundary, high above on the slopes of Plynlimon. Once empty but for sheep and derelict lead mines, the renewable forest resource now spans 30km². Whilst producing valuable timber for the manufacture of construction products, fencing, pallets, chipboard and medium-density fibreboard, Natural Resources Wales manages the Welsh Assembly Government woodlands for wildlife, archaeological conservation and the recreational demands enjoyed by its visitors.

Motorsport events and harvesting operations in the forest may affect the use of certain trails. Phone 0300 065 3000 or visit **www. naturalresources. wales** for details.

◄ Enter the forest through a gate leading on to a wide forest road (SN 828 868).

The remains of **Nant-yr-Eira Mine** on the Afon Hore are below the road to the left, but can no longer be seen due to tree growth. In the late 19th century 33 tonnes of lead were recovered from the old Bronze Age open cut mineworkings and more from the many shafts and levels.

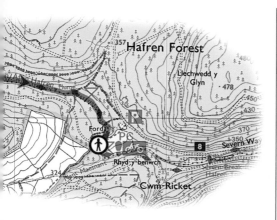

Follow the track downhill along a series of wide sweeping bends to a junction. Turn left and follow the track down to a bridge over the **Afon Hore**. Turn immediately right (SN 831 869) and take a stony path that follows the Afon Hore downstream. ▶ The river tumbles through rocks and in about 1.6km merges with the **River Severn** (Afon Hafren). Notice the small streams passing under the path which show clear signs of coming through copper-bearing strata, being stained bright orange.

Turn left along the banks of the River Severn and after about 200m cross a bridge (SN 845 874) and join the route of the Severn Way. ▶

Turn right once over the bridge and follow the River Severn, passing a flume and reaching an area with picnic tables from where a boardwalk continues downstream. At the end of the boardwalk go straight ahead up a surfaced path and zigzag up to **Rhyd-y-benwch** car park. Here toilets, picnic tables, interesting wooden sculptures and a boulder stone brought from Chepstow will help you celebrate the end of the Wye Valley Walk! You may have arranged a lift from here, but if not the Severn Way will take you into the market town of Llanidloes (see Leaving the Walk).

This is one of a number of excellent trails that have been developed in the forest, under the co-ordination of Natural Resources Wales.

The Severn Way is the longest riverside walk in Britain: 338km from its source on Plynlimon to the mouth of the Severn at Bristol.

*Rhyd-y-benwch
(Michael Mable)*

The last stamp for your Wye Valley Walk Passport is attached to an information panel. Do not forget to return your passport to receive your badge and certificate for completing the Walk (see Introduction).

Leaving the Walk
Rhyd-y-benwch to Llanidloes

OS map	Explorer 214 Llanidloes & Newtown
Public transport	
from Llanidloes	National Express bus Aberystwyth to Birmingham and London passes through Llangurig (Black Lion/post office) and Llanidloes (Gro car park); only at specified stops, book in advance. Daily Llanidloes-to-Aberystwyth bus (except Suns/public holidays. Twice-daily bus between Llanidloes, Llangurig and Rhayader (except Suns/public holidays). Regular bus Llanidloes to Caersws and Newtown where there are railway stations.
Note	The maps for this stage of the route are at half the scale of the other maps in this guide at 1:50,000.

The end of the Walk is nearly 13km (8 miles) from the nearest town of Llanidloes. There is no public transport between the two locations and although there are seasonal toilets at Rhyd-y-benwch (Hafren Forest) there are no accommodation or refreshment facilities.

It is strongly recommended that you make forward arrangements either to be collected by friends at the end of the Walk or to arrange with a local taxi company to pick you up at Rhyd-y-benwch. Please note there are no telephone facilities at Rhyd-y-benwch and no mobile phone reception. It is not recommended that you leave vehicles overnight at Rhyd-y-benwch.

If you wish to walk to Llanidloes, follow the Severn Way waymarks downstream or simply follow the road out of the picnic area; both ways eventually meet up and continue to the town along minor roads.

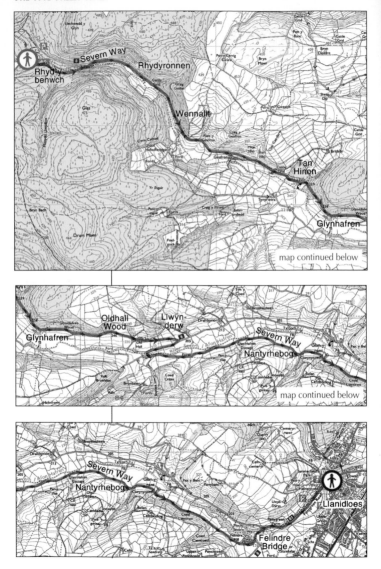

map continued below

map continued below

APPENDIX A
Route Summary and suggested itineraries

The stages described in this guide can be used as the basis for various itineraries. As well as summarising each stage, this table indicates when the **finish** of a particular stage would be a good stop on a 7-day or 10-day itinerary (averaging 19 and 13½ miles a day respectively). Don't forget to build in a rest day or two and remember to plan how you will reach Llanidloes!

Stage	Start	Finish	7-day stops	10-day stops	km	miles
1	Chepstow	Tintern			9.2	5¾
2	Tintern	Monmouth	✔	✔	16.5	10¼
3	Monmouth	Symonds Yat			8.8	5½
4	Symonds Yat	Kerne Bridge		✔	12.3	7½
5	Kerne Bridge	Ross-on-Wye	✔		8.7	5½
6	Ross-on-Wye	Fownhope		✔	17.2	10½
7	Fownhope	Hereford	✔		11	6¾
8	Hereford	Byford		✔	15.6	9¾
9	Byford	Bredwardine			7.7	4¾
10	Bredwardine	Hay-on-Wye	✔	✔	13.6	8½
11	Hay-on-Wye	Glasbury			7.7	4¾
12	Glasbury	Erwood		✔	14	8¾
13	Erwood	Builth Wells	✔		11.6	7¼
14	Builth Wells	Newbridge-on-Wye		✔	10.8	6¾
15	Newbridge-on-Wye	Rhayader	✔	✔	15.5	9½
16	Rhayader	Llangurig		✔	19.4	12
17	Llangurig	Rhyd-y-benwch	✔	✔	19.6	12¼
		TOTAL			**217.6**	**136**
Leaving the Walk						
	Rhyd-y-benwch	Llanidloes			13	8

APPENDIX B
Tourist information and advice

Due to ongoing local authority cutbacks many tourist information centres are being closed or handed to local organisations to run independently. As as a result opening hours may vary, so call in advance to check current details. The information below was correct at time of going to press but please check www.wyevalleywalk.org.uk for the most up-to-date details on tourist information, accommodation and public transport.

Other useful information for visitors can be found at:

www.visitmonmouthshire.com
www.wyedeantourism.co.uk
www.visitherefordshire.co.uk
www.visitpowys.co.uk
www.midwalesmyway.com

Chepstow TIC
Castle Car Park
Bridge Street
Chepstow NP16 5EY
Open daily, 10–5 summer, 10–3 winter
Tel: 01291 623772
Fax: 01291 628004
chepstow.tic@monmouthshire.co.uk

Old Station Visitor Info Point
Tintern NP16 7NX
Open daily: April–October
Tel: 01291 689566
oldstationtintern@monmouthshire.gov.uk

Shire Hall Visitor Info Point
Agincourt Square
Monmouth NP15 3DY
Usually open 10–4 Monday–Saturday
Tel: 01600 775257
shirehall@monmouthshire.gov.uk

Ross-on-Wye
Visitor Information Points are situated at:

Mandy Moo's
Cantilupe Road
Tel: 01989 769454

Return to Splendour
Gloucester Road
Tel: 01989 769905

Made in Ross
First floor of the Market House
Tel: 01989 769398

Raglan House Café
Broad Street
Tel: 01989 763454

Hereford Tourist Info Kiosk
Buttermarket
High Town
Hereford HR1 2AA
Open Monday–Saturday, 10–4
Tel: 01432 370514

Hay-on-Wye Tourist Information Bureau
Oxford Road
Hay-on-Wye HR3 5DG
Open daily in summer. Winter hours vary
Tel: 01497 820144
post@hay-on-wye.co.uk

Visitor Information at Rhayader Museum & Gallery
Tel: 01597 810561
info@rhayader.co.uk
Open Tues–Fri 10–4, Sat 10–1
Closed mid December to mid February

APPENDIX C
Accommodation and public transport

Accommodation
Accommodation information along the Walk is available in the form of a searchable online database on the official Walk website at www.wyevalleywalk.org.

Public Transport
Public transport information is available from National Traveline
Tel: 0871 200 22 33
www.traveline.org.uk

Information on local bus and rail services can be obtained from the relevant local authorities or Tourist Information Centres.
Railway stations can be found at Chepstow, Hereford and Builth Road (near Builth Wells).

National Rail
Tel: 03457 484950
www.nationalrail.co.uk

National Express Coach Services
Tel: 0871 7818181
www.nationalexpress.com

Local Business
Please try to support local businesses. Every purchase you make during your stay or on your Walk will help local employment and preserve jobs in the countryside. Use shops, public transport and accommodation services along the route wherever you are able.

Feedback
The local authorities who manage and maintain the Wye Valley Walk welcome your feedback – good and bad. Your comments on the attached/enclosed feedback form will help us make sure we are providing a satisfactory and enjoyable Walk. When reporting problems please provide as much information as possible about the location, ideally with photographs, a photocopied map or grid reference.
Complaints or praise can be emailed to information@wyevalleyaonb.org.uk or sent to the Information Officer, Wye Valley AONB, Hadnock Road, Monmouth NP25 3NG.

To report a problem on the route in Monmouthshire go to www.access.monmouthshire.gov.uk.

To report a problem on the route in Gloucestershire go to www.gloucestershire.gov.uk/roads-parking-and-rights-of-way/public-rights-of-way.

To report a problem on the route in Herefordshire go to http://myaccount.herefordshire.gov.uk/report-a-public-right-of-way-problem.

To report a problem on the route in Powys go to www.powys.gov.uk/en/countryside-outdoors/report-a-concern-with-a-right-of-way.

Wye Valley Walk website
For news, events, attractions, accommodation details and route updates, plus circular and easy access walks, visit the official Wye Valley Walk website www.wyevalleywalk.org.

APPENDIX D
Suggestions for circular walks

If you're interested in taking a diversion from the main path and exploring the local countryside, (or if you just want to try a shorter local walk) there is a range of circular loop walks which link to the Wye Valley Walk.

In Monmouthshire they include:

- St Arvans Roundabout
- Piercefield
- Tintern to Penterry
- Llandogo Village
- Redbrook to Penallt
- Monmouth to Redbrook
- The Angidy Trail
- Picturesque Piercefield
- Tread & Trot trails
- Whitestone – Bargain Wood – Whitestone

Details of the Monmouthshire routes can be downloaded and printed from www.visitmonmouthshire.com/walking

In Herefordshire suggested circular loop walks include:

- Leys Hill
- John Kyrle Circular, Ross-on-Wye
- Breinton Springs
- Hoarwithy
- Capler
- The Mordiford Loop

Details of all the Herefordshire routes can be downloaded and printed from the county council website at www.herefordshire.gov.uk/circularwalks.

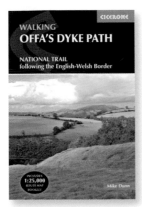

Walking – Trekking – Mountaineering – Climbing – Cycling

Over 40 years, Cicerone have built up an outstanding collection of over 300 guides, inspiring all sorts of amazing adventures.

Every guide comes from extensive exploration and research by our expert authors, all with a passion for their subjects. They are frequently praised, endorsed and used by clubs, instructors and outdoor organisations.

All our titles can now be bought as **e-books**, **ePubs** and **Kindle** files and we also have an online magazine – **Cicerone Extra** – with features to help cyclists, climbers, walkers and trekkers choose their next adventure, at home or abroad.

Our website shows any **new information** we've had in since a book was published. Please do let us know if you find anything has changed, so that we can publish the latest details. On our **website** you'll also find great ideas and lots of detailed information about what's inside every guide and you can buy **individual routes** from many of them online.

It's easy to keep in touch with what's going on at Cicerone by getting our monthly **free e-newsletter**, which is full of offers, competitions, up-to-date information and topical articles. You can subscribe on our home page and also follow us on **Facebook** and **Twitter** or dip into our **blog**.

Cicerone – the very best guides for exploring the world.

CICERONE

Juniper House, Murley Moss, Oxenholme Road, Kendal, Cumbria LA9 7RL
Tel: 015395 62069 info@cicerone.co.uk
www.cicerone.co.uk and **www.cicerone-extra.com**

WYE VALLEY WALK PASSPORT

Chepstow	Redbrook
Symonds Yat	Ross on Wye
Mordiford	Hereford
Brewardine	Hay on Wye
Erwood	Builth

Rhayader	Gilfach
Llangurig	Hafren Forest

COLLECT A RECORD OF YOUR WALK AT THE WVW STAMPING POINTS

Why not keep a record of your journey along the **Wye Valley Walk** by collecting stamps at up to 14 key locations on this passport? Once you have six stamps, including both Chepstow and Hafren Forest, you can send for your exclusive badge and completion certificate. (Stamping station opening hours vary and locations can change so please check www.wyevalley.org for the latest information.)

Send your completed passport to:
The Wye Valley Walk Partnership
Wye Valley AONB Office, Hadnock Road, Monmouth NP25 3NG

(You can also get extra passports for fellow walkers before you start, by writing to this address, emailing information@wyevalleyaonb.org.uk or calling 01600 710846.)

Name...

Address..

....

....

Postcode..

Please tick if you would like this card returned

with your badge and certificate. ☐

WYE VALLEY WALK FEEDBACK FORM

To help us maintain the highest standards for the Wye Valley Walk we would be grateful if you could take the time to answer the following questions to let us know about your experience of the walk and whether you encountered any difficulties along the way. When you have finished, you can return it to us using the Freepost address overleaf.

When did you do the Walk? ....

How many days did it take? ....

Where did you start the Walk ? ....

Where did you finish the Walk? ....

How many people were in your party? ....

adults .... children ....

Did you have any dogs with you? If so, how many? ....

What was your overall experience of the walk (please tick one)?

very good ☐   good ☐   fair ☐   poor ☐   very poor ☐

Roughly, how much did your party spend while doing the Wye Valley Walk

...on accommodation? £ ....

...on food and refreshments? £ ....

...on transport? £ ....

Were any in your party mobility-impaired? Yes ☐ No ☐

If so, did they encounter any difficulties with the Walk (please describe below, giving grid references if possible for particular locations)

....

....

How did you hear about the Walk?..

Where did you buy this guide?...

How do you think we could improve the Walk? (please give grid references if possible for particular locations)

....

....

Your name ....

Your postal address..

....

Telephone number..

Email address ....

Please return this form to: **Wye Valley AONB Office**, FREEPOST SWC 4106, Monmouth NP25 3ZZ.

Thank you for taking the time to help us make the Wye Valley Walk as enjoyable and accessible as possible for all our visitors.